UNDERSTANDING
MALE SEXUAL ABUSE

UNDERSTANDING MALE SEXUAL ABUSE

WHY MALE VICTIMS REMAIN SILENT

O'BRIEN DENNIS

Foreword by Sonia Haynes, MS,
Certified School Psychologist, New York City

iUniverse, Inc.
Bloomington

Understanding Male Sexual Abuse
Why Male Victims Remain Silent

iUniverse books may be ordered through booksellers or by contacting:

iUniverse
1663 Liberty Drive
Bloomington, IN 47403
www.iuniverse.com
1-800-Authors (1-800-288-4677)

ISBN: 978-1-4620-1696-9 (sc)
ISBN: 978-1-4620-1695-2 (hc)
ISBN: 978-1-4620-1694-5 (ebk)

Library of Congress Control Number: 2011915116

Printed in the United States of America

iUniverse rev. date: 10/05/2011

Contents

To all who helped to make this work possible and continue to believe in me. In the memory of Sylvie Cameron, for without her help and encouragement my dream would not have become a reality.

When your life is on course with its purpose, you are your most powerful. With every challenging experience there's an opportunity to grow, enhance your life, or learn something invaluable about yourself.

—Oprah Winfrey

Preface

Names in this book of those who share their stories, which are all true, have been changed in order to protect their identities.

Their stories were documented by the survivors in their authentic voices, and these personal stories were written in the emotional language of the victims. I edited them to correct grammar and punctuation when it was important for the sake of clarity.

Given the ever-changing nature of the Internet, any web address or links contained in this book may have changed since publication and may no longer be valid.

The views expressed in this work are solely those of the author. The author, while he has done extensive research on male sexual abuse, is not a fully trained researcher and is by no means attempting to draw scientific conclusion from this work. The views of the author do not necessarily reflect the views of the publisher. The publisher does not assume any responsibility for the views or opinion mentioned in this book.

Acknowledgments

I take this opportunity to first and foremost show my gratitude to Professor Benjamin Sher, who was my constructive-action instructor at the Metropolitan College of New York (MCNY). This book would not have been possible if it were not for his guidance and patience. In addition, the faculty at MCNY played a huge role in my advancement; their knowledge of the social service and business worlds opened my eyes to an endless set of opportunities. I thank my fellow classmates, the masters in public administration class of 2009. Special recognition must be given to Sylvie Cameron, my academic advisor in whose memory this book is dedicated, who saw more in me than I saw in myself; I could always count on her support and creative mind to push me toward believing and achieving my dream.

Special thanks to the dedicated staff and community researchers at New York City Alliance Against Sexual Assault and all those who work on Project ENVISION. Thanks to those pillars of support, Chris and Beth Ann, and the team at the Bronx District Attorney's Office. A special thanks to the many people from around the world I met at the 2010 Male Survivors conference held at John Jay College in New York City. I received a better understanding of male sexual abuse from a global perspective, and it redirected the outline of this book.

To all my friends who have been supportive, patient, and understanding, especially when I had little or no time for them.

I cannot forget the men who were brave enough to share their stories with me. Without them, this work would not be possible. I am greatly indebted to you all for your courage and strength. It is your voices that have shaped this work, and it is your stories that will leave a lasting impression on all who read this book.

I would also like to take the opportunity to thank my coworkers for taking part in the questionnaire section and for M. E. C. for believing in me, the work I have ahead of me, and for giving me some of the best counseling a man could get. Thank you for your patience and understanding, and ignoring me when my mind was obviously elsewhere.

When no one seemed to believe in me, exceptional thanks goes to Sonia Haynes for writing the foreword.

The final product could not have become a reality without the help of Antoine Graigwell, who for the second time around kept nightly vigils with me to go through the book and guide me to the changes that were needed. Nuff love and respect for being one of my biggest supporters.

To the friends I have lost along the way, especially Grimaldo Medrano; you are forever missed.

Deepest gratitude to the two most important men in my life—the two who have shared my pain and my struggles; endured my hardships with me; and given me unconditional love, support, and friendship. The world is a much better place because of you both; from the beginning, you saw the dream, lived my dream, and kept me in check when my world was no longer in balance.

To my partner, who has given me unconditional love, even when I was not deserving of it. It is the love you showed me that helped me to realize I can trust again.

Finally, to my immediate family, who are supportive and understanding in allowing me to once again deal with my past and pain in such a public forum.

Foreword

By Sonia Haynes, MS
Certified School Psychologist
New York City

Childhood sex abuse is often an undiscussed subject. Children are often ashamed or feel as if they deserved what happened to them, and many carry the guilt of feeling they encouraged their abuser. It can take many years for someone to open up about his or her abuse; many never tell their stories. While in as many as 93 percent of sex abuse cases the victims know the perpetrator and while 63 percent are family members, an estimated 88 percent of abuse cases are never reported.

I have seen many children and their families destroyed by "the secret." Many children often blame themselves and then lead destructive lives so as not to face their feelings of shame and guilt. Children who experience child abuse and neglect are 59 percent more likely to get arrested as a juvenile, 28 percent more likely to be arrested as an adult, and 30 percent more likely to commit a violent crime.

Too often, people will not speak about their past for fear of rejection. In my experience as a certified school psychologist, I have worked with many children and young adults who do not want to disclose the history of their sexual abuse. Most feared disclosure because the abusers were family members; others felt they "deserved it." The hardest part of working with these children and young adults is helping them understand that abuse is unacceptable and that speaking out about it does not make them any "less of a person."

I applaud O'Brien Dennis for having the courage to be open about his experience of abuse. It takes a great amount of strength and is a tremendous accomplishment to not only survive but to tell your story as well. His first book, *The Cries of Men: Voices of Jamaican Men Who Have Been Raped and Sexually Abused*, was inspiring. I have recommended it to many clinicians, suggesting they read his story and use it as an example with their clients. After reading his book, I realized that there are many more people out there who are suffering at the hands of people who say they care but really do not, and as a result, the victims are afraid to tell. While the statistics show that girls are more often abused than boys, the tendency of boys and men to not to report their victimizations may affect these statistics.

The emotional trauma associated with abuse is likely to swing from one extreme to another. This can lead children and young adults to exhibit maladaptive behaviors. Many children likely suffer from a range of psychological and behavioral problems from mild to severe and from short term to long term. These problems typically include depression, anxiety, and inappropriate sexual interests, which many carry with them into adulthood.

Men and women who have suffered sexual abuse have deep emotional scars. Some abused children are likely to be ongoing victims, falling prey to others. Most will not receive any assistance from others, not because people do not care, but because they feel it may be none of their business. While there are many treatment facilities for abused children and young adults, one who is the victim of abuse must be willing to seek out this assistance. Telling your story is the first and hardest step. Once you take that step, it will open up a whole new world where you can feel free. It is important to remember the effects of sexual abuse. It is also important that clinicians as well as lay people not judge someone who was abused. Being abused, especially as a child or in prison, is not something a person encourages, rather it is something for which the abuser or perpetrator should be ashamed. Sexual abuse is a crime that has to be handled delicately and discreetly so to avoid turning the spotlight on the victim.

Dennis's ability to tell his story and explore the other areas of sexual abuse in this book open up a whole new opportunity for him to help others. Undoubtedly, this new book is likely to provide assistance to others who would not be able to understand what sex abuse is and to whom it can happen. It may assist others in understanding why many people do not report their abuse and inspire many others who are suffering in silence.

Introduction

Following the publication of my book *The Cries of Men: Voices of Jamaican Men Who Have Been Raped and Sexually Abused,* many people wanted me to write a follow-up to my story. That was going to be difficult, simply because I had already told my story and there wasn't much left to be said about my life. Often, as I did book readings and presentations about male sexual abuse, I realized that many people still didn't fully understand the scope and ripple effects of the problem, and how male sexual abuse impacted our daily lives both directly and indirectly. Definitively, this isn't a continuation of *The Cries of Men*.

While doing my thesis topic "Understanding Male Sexual Abuse" for the masters-degree program I undertook in 2009, I was expected to create a constructive action plan, which meant I had to find an organization, do a SWOT analysis (a strategic planning method used to evaluate the Strengths, Weaknesses, Opportunities, and Threats involved in a project or in an organization) of the organization, and create an action plan to solve a particular problem. At the time, I was privileged to be working with the New York City Alliance Against Sexual Abuse, and they agreed that I could focus on their organization, identify a problem, and implement an action plan to resolve what I found. My internship, also part of the masters program, allowed for me to be trained as a researcher with Project ENVISION.

The Alliance, in conjunction with eleven of New York City's rape-crisis programs, is implementing a six-year, citywide project to prevent sexual violence. The goal of Project ENVISION is to change the social norms that promote and permit sexual violence in the city so that there is a reduction in sexual violence. One approach to such a multilevel change is community mobilization, which involves organizing communities for the purpose of developing and implementing programs that are tailored to a specific issue. The success of this project hinges on bringing together various segments or sectors of each of the communities involved in the demonstration project so that they can work together to analyze the causes and effects of sexual violence within their communities and to pool resources for design and action.

While I enjoyed working on Project ENVISION and I am grateful for the abundance of knowledge and skill sets that I learned, I realized that ENVISION only revolved around female sexual abuse. On many occasions, in formal and informal discussions, I expressed a strong opposition to the feminist approach to solveing sexual violence. My vision was to research male and female sexual abuse. I felt it was pointless to ignore the reality that men are sexually abused, especially with the media being caught up in the child sex-abuse scandals in the Roman Catholic Church. I could neither continue with pure conscience, nor could I be a hypocrite. Up against many brick walls at ENVISION, I decided to walk away from that experience and refocused my energies on conducting an independent study of understanding male sexual abuse. Using *The Cries of Men* as my platform, I decided to let society have a better understanding of male sexual abuse. Out of this emerged another part of my vision, the O'Brien Dennis Foundation.

The O'Brien Dennis Foundation was launched in the fall of 2009. It was born of a need to conduct research into male sexual abuse by using the well-established feminist approach and to give men an outlet to cope with their abuse. The foundation has passed its planning stages and is currently pursuing funding opportunities to start research projects. Launching the O'Brien Dennis Foundation was not a challenge to the work of the Alliance, rather it was a means to form a coalition to get a better understanding of male sexual abuse and to work collectively to end sexual violence.

For male victims of sexual abuse, their violation has been seen as a taboo topic tainted with homosexuality and guilt and shame. The lack of understanding of what causes a man to sexually abuse another male and society's age-old definition of masculinity have left so many male victims voiceless. In society's narrow definition of masculinity, men find it difficult to cope with male-on-male sexual abuse. Through research, I was able to gather enough information to prove that male sexual abuse is significantly underreported and undertreated. The relaunch of *The Cries of Men*, which is an autobiographical account of rape, was used as the guiding tool for this research. Finally, the public was able to put a face to the problem and listen to the voice of one who survived and who was brave enough to say "it happened to me." The research is helping to change social perceptions about male sexual abuse, and finally a voice is being given to the subject. Dialogue is beginning to open up, and empathy towards male victims is building. The product will be a research-driven foundation, which will continue delving into the many issues surrounding male sexual abuse and how to bring about meaningful change.

Following the 2010 Male Survivors conference, I decided to gather more stories to take this out of the realm of academia and to make this book more readable by a wider cross section. I felt that it was important to have male survivors share their stories in their own voices in order to allow readers to better understand how these victims and survivors coped with the abuse. To provide readers with an opportunity to understand my passion and what has driven me along this path, I decided in the first chapter to recount my own personal story and survival of sexual abuse. As my story unfolds, readers will be better able to understand why I never sought help and why I remained silent for so many years. This book contains testimonies from men who, before sharing their stories, were voiceless. For their own health and healing and to help others who are suffering in silence, it is imperative that their stories be relayed authentically in their own language.

The stories of these men that you are about to read are real, and I hope that by learning more about each individual story you as the reader will get a better understanding of male sexual abuse and possibly change your perception about male sexual abuse.

To supplement these intimate stories with a more comprehensive context, I decided to study the academic research on understanding of male sexual abuse and male survivors, and I have included some of my findings in the following chapters, not as a formal research paper into the secondary sources on the topic, but rather as information that will also help the reader come to a clearer understanding of male sexual abuse.

The conversation on male sexual abuse does not end after reading this book—more research needs to be done to take an ecological approach to understanding male sexual abuse and how it impacts society. Change comes only when we first acknowledge and accept there is a problem. In my research, I have not come across any correlations between male sexual abuse and homosexuality. But a tendency toward homosexuality is likely to continue to rise on those occasions when and where men engage in same-sex encounters as a means to cope with or get a better understanding of who they are. While not much research has been done into the ripple effects of male sexual abuse, some studies have shown that there is a direct connection between male sexual abuse, alcohol addiction, drug abuse, sexual promiscuity, the spread of sexually transmitted diseases, and the alarming rate of HIV infection, especially within communities populated by people of color.

As I approached the end of writing the book in the fall of 2010, Oprah Winfrey teamed up with movie producer Tyler Perry and hosted a two-day event, during which two hundred men who were sexually abused as children told their stories and spoke their truths. The show spoke about the healing process of coming forward and verbalizing that these men were sexually abused and how cathartic was that acknowledgement. This was a seminal opportunity for society to see and understand that male sexual abuse happens and to hear from these men how their lives were affected. The men spoke about the aftermath of sexual abuse, depression, coping with the abuse, troubled relationships, intimacy issues, sexual confusion, and the stigma that surrounded male sexual abuse.

Dr. Howard Fradkin, a psychologist and a member of Male Survivors, who has dedicated his career to helping male survivors noted, "It takes a lot of time. It impacts everybody in your life because you don't want to talk. You don't want to share. You don't want to trust that anyone will honor the very things that you've had to keep inside for so long."

At the end of the first show, I decided to post a Facebook request for men to join my cause and tell their story. The feedback was astounding, and I got the opportunity to start the conversation among my friends on using social networking. As a result of that show, I was energized and more focused on playing my role in helping to end sexual abuse.

The stories that you will read in his book are intended to show that male sexual abuse has no boundaries, no racial, ethnic, or color lines; it transcends religious or cultural lines. Anyone can be a victim and many are survivors; wherever humans exist, sexual abuse has no regard for geographical or social upbringing.

Chapter 1

Three Rapes Occurring in Darkness

Maturity comes when we have acknowledged and accepted that we have little or no control over our past and when we have accepted the things we have little or no control over.

I still have issues sleeping, and while I have not been professionally diagnosed with sleep apnea, I understand what it's like to have a consistently interrupted sleep pattern. To explain the background of this dysfunctional sleep pattern, I have to return to my childhood, which I do not recall with many fond memories. Then and as I grew older, most of my thoughts were consumed by one of my best kept secrets. I was five-years old when my childhood was taken from me. As a male child in a rural community in Jamaica, I grew up with no affirmations from adults of my self worth: I believed I was unattractive and I didn't deserve love. Today, I still struggle with the fear of loving someone and not having that love returned.

Through listening to others speak of their abuse, I have come to realize that my story is not unique, and the pain I kept locked up inside wasn't restricted to Jamaica, the touristy Caribbean island paradise.

Recently, while shopping in a Caribbean market close by where I live in Westchester, New York, I encountered an item that encapsulated my past; it had trapped me in silence and pain for more than twenty-five years. As I passed by the fruit section and an assortment of Jamaican sodas, out of the corner of my eye I saw the familiar orange color of carbolic soap. Even though I was not close, its unmistakable smell invaded my nose, assaulting my olfactory senses either with its real presence or from the memories stored in my mind. It was a smell I knew only too well from years ago. The memory of the experience overpowered me; I ran out of the grocery store, tears streaming down my face.

Even though I am unable to completely relive that horrific experience, I often have moments when for reasons unknown, details of the bathroom, the act, and of my abuser, flash in my mind as a single image. I have since realized that because of the shower experience as a child, I hate taking showers, especially to have the water flow over my face. Ironically, I realize that the association with sex and a shower is why I have such a strong passion for having sex in the shower. The fear of reliving my past has kept my mind imprisoned and prevented me from truly dealing with what had happened. I could not believe that, twenty years later, I still had vivid memories of the event that changed my life. I was trying to cope, but it was never easy, especially when I was alone.

Up to the time of the abuse when I was a five-year old, I was a very vibrant, talkative child who was adored by everyone. I had a sense that I was loved. As a sign of the favoritism in my family, my uncle called me Rossi, after Paolo Rossi, who in 1982 led Italy in the 1982 FIFA World Cup. While I enjoy being a spectator, I am far from good at the game. I was always an inquisitive child growing up, and my curiosity later got the best of me. While I lived with my grandmother in Westmoreland, often I would visit my mother who had moved to live and work in August Town a part of Kingston, the capital of Jamaica.

On a warm, summer evening in 1985, while spending the weekend with my grandmother, my innocence was taken away from me. I was passing the communal shower in the neighborhood when I saw my neighbor's sixteen-year-old son taking a shower. He called me to him, and curious about what he wanted, I went over. I recall as if it happened yesterday—he asked me to come into the shower stall with him. Even today, I could still see the image in my mind of him lathering his body with soap and spending a long time with the soap in his hands on his genitals. I cannot forget the smell of the carbolic soap he used to lather himself.

I was clueless as to what had occurred to me in the shower. I only knew that it never felt right, and I should never tell anyone about what had happened. It all took place so fast, and it was nonverbal. I had no clue what sex was or that someone took advantage of me or the fact that my innocence was taken away from me. Even without my abuser telling me what my next move should be, I knew then that if I said anything, no one would have believed me. I now realized why I had so many horrible nightmares as a child: I was fearful of not being believed. I felt what had happened was my fault, and no one would believe a child.

My grandmother was the one person I wanted to tell, but she died before I managed to tell her about the experience. I knew she saw the pain in my eyes and my subdued behavior. I knew she wondered what had happened, but she didn't ask. She never knew how to find the words to start that kind of conversation. I was close to her and disappointing her was the furthest thing from my mind. So, I kept this secret to myself. Today, I feel sad that I didn't have the strength and courage and was unable to tell her what had been done to me.

Following the experience with the neighbor in the shower, I became secretive. At nights, I felt that aliens would come and take me away simply because I was not a good boy. Not only did I lose that childhood innocence, I lost my smile and my spirit—my joy for life. When I look at any of my childhood pictures, I was never smiling in any of them. I never felt happy, because I knew that I was different. Someone had made me different, and I grew up believing that it was my fault. I never seemed to fit in. I was always a loner, and I constantly looked at myself in mirrors, trying to reassure myself that I was still a child.

I now work with children who have serious emotional and developmental challenges, and when I looked at a photograph of me from a high-school year book a friend posted on Facebook, I saw the familiar sadness and disinterest in my facial expression. Oddly enough, no one saw then what was going on, and no one even took the time to inquire. To numb the pain and the depression I felt, I started drinking. From as early as eleven or twelve-years-old I drank a mixture of Jamaican white rum and orange juice, which I kept in a small ice cooler. It was all I needed to get through each day.

For the remainder of my childhood, I was withdrawn and morose. But, as if once was not enough, when I was fourteen years old, I was again set upon, and this time by a twenty-one-year old neighbor who worked setting up electronic systems. He had seen me having sex with another fourteen-year-old schoolmate, and thought to use what he had seen as a tool to blackmail me into having sex with him. At the time, I was having difficulty with my school work, and when he approached me more friendly than he had been before, I told him of my plight. He offered to help tutor me and a quasi-friendship began to develop. Then some time later, he reminded me of the his threat to tell my mother of what he had seen, unless I gave in to his demands to have him penetrate me.

After several months of helping me with my school work and being a mentor, trust developed between us. When he asked me again about having sex with him, I refused. One night, when I was over at his house so he could help me with my school work, he forced himself on me, pinned me down, and raped me to the sound track from the movie *Waiting to Exhale*. During the experience when he took advantage of me, several tunes played on his CD player, including Mary J. Blige's "Not Gon' Cry" and Patti LaBelle's "My Love, Sweet Love."

I will never forget that night for as long as I live. It took years before I could ever listen to that sound track and relive the memories of that horrifying night. These songs will always remain with me. They will always be a part of me

After my abuser, who I had miscast as my mentor, had violated me, he held me in his arms as a mother would a child. I went home that night bleeding, ashamed, afraid, and filled with guilt. I had no one to talk to. I was the child; he was the adult. Who would have believed me? The fear of no one believing me is one of the reasons I kept silent for so long—also, it was the fear of believing that I asked for it and, more importantly, that the act itself had turned me into a homosexual.

I cried myself to sleep that night, and I went to school the following day with tissue paper between my butt cheeks to stop the bleeding. How would I start the conversation? How could I find the words to tell even my best friend what had happened to me the previous night? I started doubting myself; who I was. I convinced myself that the abuse was my fault.

Going to the police was never an option; not even a possibility. I knew what would happen. Jamaica is known everywhere as one of the most homophobic countries in the world, where anyone, male or female, suspected of or caught in any same-sex act or relationship is dealt with harshly by both the authorities and citizenry alike. I was more afraid of what the police would do to me than I was of being disbelieved.

Days after the rape, I went back to my abuser, asking him why he did it. I had come to believe that he was the only person I felt comfortable talking to, and the weirdest thing was, I still trusted him. I believed in all that he had done for me before the assault, and I felt indebted to him for all the help he had given to me to improve my grades. As consolation, my mentor told me that if it would make me feel comfortable I could do what he had done to me. With the same music, the sounds of Whitney Houston's "Waiting to Exhale" playing on his CD player, I did what I was instructed to do and performed as commanded. After it ended, I felt as if I had erased what had happened to me that night before. That night was the first of many sexual encounters that helped not only to mess up my mental frame of mind, but defined what love shouldn't be.

For two years, I engaged in a sexual relationship with my abuser. I felt loved, desired, cared for, nurtured, and, most importantly, confident that the relationship would last a lifetime. But it has had a detrimental effect on all my future relationships: I lost trust and confidence in anyone who has come into my life and who has loved me unconditionally. I still struggle with trust and boundary issues, and too often I am unable to differentiate between sex and love.

Without warning, as if he had picked a fruit, eaten it, and now was ready to discard the skin and pits, he abruptly ended our sexual liaison.

When I completed high school I transitioned to attending a community college some distance from my home in order to prepare for university. My family never understood my reasons for not wanting to go to a community college closer to home. Instead, for two years I attended a college deep in the interior of the island. My drinking, which had started early in my childhood and which had continued unabated, increased significantly.

Also, I engaged in random and risky sexual encounters, including having sex with another roommate at the same time when our apartment also housed several fellow students. In the Jamaican culture, if we were caught or suspicions aroused, we could have been killed. I used both sex and alcohol to mask the pain I was going through and to cope with the rigors of college. I did everything I could do to stay from home, and I never had much of a desire to return. I was accepted to the University of the West Indies, Mona Campus, when I completed community college. Until this point,, I could barely function or manage my school work, now, in university with little or no supervision, I was left to fend for myself.

With the independence of being alone at university came a desire to search for answers to why the man I had trusted and believed in so much had hurt me: I came to realize that he no longer wanted me. I also wanted to know if there was something about me that was odd—the way I walked, the way I carried myself, did I telegraph some signal? I internalized all of my emotions. And, because of my lack of understanding, I neglected the one thing I had set out to do, gain an education. I had set myself up to fail.

My life was not without some happy moments. A three year stretch, between 1998 and 2001, were some of the best years of my life. I met many people who played an instrumental role in shaping who I am today. During this period I learned how to define myself, and I forged a group of friendships that continue to sustain me.

In the pursuit of answers and identifying with others like myself, I met a young man online named Chris, and we developed a friendship, even though it was at a distance. Like every relationship, it had components of trust, which seemed to defy the odds.

It felt good knowing that I was finally able to talk to someone who knew where I was coming from and who understood the pain I was going through. The friendship was platonic and long distance, and it gave me hope that I could once again trust someone. I still had my struggles with trust and felt comfortable only communicating by phone or through the Internet.

After months of constant pleading from him, I agreed to meet Chris for the first time the weekend before my finals. He asked if he could bring a friend to the meeting—an older man—and I didn't object.

The meeting and the subsequent encounter happened, as had my previous bad experiences, on dark night. At the time across the entire island, there were rolling blackouts. The government said they were trying to save energy. In Kingston, the blackout and the buildings made the streets seem darker. Chris, his friend, and I went to a neighborhood outside of the city to the friend's house. By the time we arrived, the electricity had returned. The night itself was balmy—a cool, moisture-laden night, overcast with clouds—and no stars were visible. I was curious to see what would develop. But, what happened that dark, moonless night became part of the mosaic of other images and experiences that are indelibly impressed in my mind.

Chris's friend, whose name I never got, was an older man of about forty-five years. Although I later found out that the older man had children, one of whom was as old as Chris and I, this encounter was the first and last time I met him. At twenty one, Chris and I were the same age. When we arrived at the older man's house, he invited Chris and me inside. At the time the BET television network was popular, and a BET show was on the television. Fascinated, I started watching the show. The older man remained with me in his living room, and we talked about life and growing up.

After a short while, he said he had heard that I was well endowed—that I had a big dick. I was taken aback by this, since as I didn't know him and Chris and I had never had any such conversations. I wasn't sure how he came to know that about me. As the conversation continued, I became aware that what he was saying grew increasingly inappropriate, but I tried to remain disengaged, waiting for Chris to reappear. After speaking with me for about fifteen minutes, the older man excused himself and left the room. I continued to wait, but after about twenty minutes I began to wonder where Chris had gone. I knew that houses such as this had only one entrance and exit, and I was standing close to the door where Chris had to pass. Wondering where he had gone, and not hearing any sounds, even of conversation, I started looking around.

I came to a bedroom door, which was open, and I saw the older man performing oral sex on Chris. The older man was seated on the edge of the bed, and Chris was standing in front of him, his back toward me, partially obscuring the older man. I guessed what they were doing and was shocked but remained transfixed in the doorway. I realized then that I had become aroused. My penis started to get hard, and I unbuttoned my pants, pushed my underwear down, and began masturbating.

After a while, Chris looked around, and when he saw me, he beckoned with a head movement for me to come over and join in. Equally in silence, with a shake of my head, I said no, and mouthed that I was okay where I stood. The two continued for another few minutes, and then the older man looked up, stopped what he was doing, and asked me to come closer.

With my pants and underwear in a bunch at my ankles, I waddled over to stand closer to them. Then, after another moment when it seemed as though I was just a spectator at an event, the older man reached out with one of his free hands—the other held Chris around his hips—and took my arm, gently pulling me closer to them. Chris reached out his arm, drew me in closer, and I stumbled and fell on the bed.

It all happened in a blur, because the next thing I knew, I was laying on my belly, my face in the bed clothes, and Chris was forcing his penis between my buttocks. I started to struggle, fighting and flailing my arms and legs in every direction and pushing my body up to get Chris off of me, but it seemed as if every time I pushed back to throw him off me, it was all he needed to push his penis more forcibly into my anus. The pain seared through my body. I tried to scream, but a hand I recognized as rough and belonging to the older man, was planted over my mouth, stifling any sound I made. Still trying to fight them off, I became aware that the older man had laid his body across my back and pinned me down and Chris was continuing to force himself into me. The more I fought, the more the pain became intense, and I drifted in an empty space, praying that it would soon all be over.

When he finished, Chris told me that this is what I had wanted. For the second time someone else was telling me what they thought I wanted. Together, Chris and the older man called a cab, put me in it and sent me back to my dorm room on the university's campus. When I returned to the dorm, I felt so abused and betrayed, once again, that if I could have only find the strength and an open window to hang myself, I would have. This time, I told myself that it was my fault, and I knew that if I told Anyone, no one would have believed. I was a grown man. I was not forced to go with them. I remember during the actual rape I became sexually aroused. My penis got hard, and in retrospect I wondered how much I became excited by the violence of the act.

In a country where homosexuality is illegal and punishable for up to ten years hard labor, going to the police would not be an option. This was when the self-destructive behavior started; this was when I no longer felt I had a meaning or purpose to live. Weeks after the rape, I ran away from Jamaica, never to return to the land I once called home. When I finally decided to report the crime, from my new residence in New York, I called the police's crime victims' unit. When I described what had happened to me to Inspector Barret from the Statistical Department of the Police Commissioner's office, a unit of the crime victims' unit, he said that, since I didn't have a vagina, it was impossible that I could have been raped.

Running away then seemed to have been an easy choice, but I never realized that I would have to find coping mechanisms to deal with the memories of the abuse, along with the shame and guilt of believing that it was my fault. I can finally admit that I have had sporadic periods of chronic depressive periods in my life, during which I did things that I have now grown to regret, in order to erase the memory of my abuse. As with a drug addict who uses drugs to get a high and possibly to forget, I used sex as my drug—to get high for a short period of time. It was just a quick fix; I was never satisfied, no matter how many sexual encounters I had.

Sexual addiction for me was just like taking hard drugs, and while I understood the consequences of my actions, I was unable to control my desires. I wanted to stop, but the more I tried to stop, the more intrigued I became by the level of attention I received from other men. The compliments about my lean body and the fact that I was able to satisfy the needs of these men enticed me the most. The attention these men gave me made me feel human, made me feel accepted in a world I felt hated me and would never accept my past and the struggles I had to endure. I would have sex anywhere, any time, and I made personal and financial sacrifices just to maintain my habit. I had that likeability factor, my youthfulness, a thick Jamaican accent, and a sex drive that was always on high.

Not only was I addicted to sex, I had a chronic alcohol addiction. It wasn't until I got older that I realized that I was a functional alcoholic. I could not go a day without drinking. My choice of liquor was Jamaican White Rum and Appleton Rum—the Appleton chilled in a freezer and drunk without any chaser. The feeling of it rushing down inside your body is like a burning fire that is out of control.

I have since learned to control my sexual appetite and I have tried to be monogamous, and since 2005, I have not touched any alcohol. Getting over my addictions was no easy task, and I am still searching for love and acceptance, most times in all the wrong places. I have learned how to forgive, to let go of the past, and to move on with my life, but the past still lingers. Every time I am asked to tell my story, the shame of what happened to me takes over, and I am deprived of any feelings of happiness.

I want to be loved, not only by my partner, who would love me unconditionally and without judgment. I yearn for the intimate love of family. The first group of people that a child interacts with is its family. They foster and develop a sense of trust and love in the child. If that trust and love is betrayed, the child—and the person the child grows to be—is left with nothing. The adult person feels emptiness deep inside and a desire to fill an empty void, which most times will not be filled. Wounds heal over time, but the scars leave a mark for life.

I struggle with the reality that so many men have found confidence and strength from me. I have been able to help so many children and their families, yet I am unable to resolve my own issues. I can give advice on love, yet I am still searching for my own love and acceptance. For however long that may take, I will continue the work that I am doing, and I will seek help so that I can obtain the skills needed to change more lives. I know for sure that God has a purpose of my survival—this is my calling and I cannot deny myself the blessings of God.

Sexual abuse of boys and men is deep and pervasive in many cultures across the world. In many closed societies or communities, as with acts of domestic violence in which husbands or wives beat up their spouses, daughters are sexually molested by male relatives. So, too, males in these families are abused. But there is an insidious silence that surrounds male abuse victims: because of the perceptions of masculinity, who would a male victim of sexual abuse turn to without feeling shame and less than a man?

Additionally, male sexual abuse victims who were courageous to step out of the shadows and report what was done to them in an effort to correct and repair their damaged lives, have revealed that their abuse is not only confined to male on male abuse, but women too commit sexual abuse against men.

Studies have revealed that across the United States close to 3 percent of men have experienced rape at some point in their lives, which translates to approximately 2.78 million men. The reluctance through shame to report male sexual abuse has prevented the compilation of accurate statistics in comparison to female sexual abuse victims, which are reported more often. A 2003 National Crime Victims Study suggested that one of every six victims is under twelve-years old. Researchers Tjaden and Thoennes in their 2006 study revealed that a staggering 71 percent of all male victims were first raped before their eighteenth birthday; 16.6 percent were between eighteen and twenty-four years old, and 12.3 percent were twenty-five years or older.

It is known that males are the least likely to report a sexual assault. Given society's narrow definition of masculinity along with presumptions of homosexuality when placed with shame and sexual identity confusion, many men find it very difficult to report the assault and seek help. Humanity's socialization process of teaching boys how to become men before their time has forced many into prisons of the mind, which has led many to become chronically depressed, engage in unsafe sexual habits, and become addicted to drugs and alcohol.

Chapter 2

History of Sexual Abuse

It is a known fact that Male rape is a taboo subject; it is pervasive in every culture yet it is concealed by the victims who are too ashamed to speak out and by societies that is not prepared to listen

Historically, in times of war, the rape of both men and women has been used as a psychological tool. The researcher Stephen Donaldson, in his article "Can We Put an End to Inmate Rape?" published in 1990, said that in ancient times the rape of males occurred more widely. Several of the legends in Greek mythology involved abduction and sexual assaults of men by other men or male gods. Historical contexts have been dominated by notions of masculinity and of male rape. In *The Cries of Men*, published in 2005, I suggested that there was a widespread belief that a male who was sexually penetrated "lost his manhood," even if it was forced sexual assault, and as such he could no longer be considered a warrior or ruler. Rape historically has been used to emasculate men to keep them servile and submissive in times of slavery. Some historians have suggested that homosexuality as an act was forced on many slaves, to keep them in submission, yet, there is no link that exists between homosexuality and male rape. Donaldson said that the rape of men was considered the ultimate form of punishment and, as such, was a penalty for adultery in Roman times and in ancient Persians for violation of the sanctity of the harem.

Based on my research and reading on the subject of sexual abuse, feminist researchers have for years argued that sexual violence is not the mere meaningless explosion of inner rage. Rather, it often involves purposeful action that is aimed at maintaining male supremacy through intimidation, abuse, and repression. The long-established feminist view of sexual abuse has failed to examine and acknowledge the fact that men are frequently and disproportionately victimized by other men with these same objectives as perpetuated on women. J. A. Tickner in, *Gender in International Relations*, published in 1992 said that in the "spoils of war" theory that supporting the need for greater protection of women in war acknowledges only one level of meaning in war: rape and other forms of sexual violence. From this theoretical foundation, other literature have meticulously explored historical texts, dating as far back as the Bible, in which women were deemed the "property" of the enemy. An effective way to challenge the enemy, therefore, is to defile his "property," that is to say, his women.

Undoubtedly, the spoils of war theory are grounded in solid historical evidence. G. A. Kelson, G. in the 1999 publication *Gender and Immigration* discusses the transcripts from the Balkans war trials, which serve to underscore as an important level of intent, expressed in modern times, using countless incidents of sexual violence against women and girls to support the spoils of war theory. Contemporary literature on rape in times of war has failed to recognize another, equally important level of intent and meaning behind sexual violence: the intent to emasculate the enemy. This is done not only by tainting the enemy's female property, but also by tarnishing the male enemy's body. The greatest humiliation a man can impose on another man or boy is that of turning him into a de facto female through sexual cruelty.

The spoils of war theory, expressed in B. Ehrenreich's 1997 *Blood Rites*, is the confiscation of the enemy's women and is as old as history itself. Ancient Persian murals show triumphant warriors bearing plates piled high with their enemy's penises. In his article, "Sexual Violence Against Men in Armed Conflict," published in 2007, Sandesh Sivakumaran notes that there are substantial evidence that indicates that sexual violence also takes place against men in armed conflicts. It is also pointed out in the article that male sexual abuse takes place in nearly every armed conflicts in which sexual violence is used as a tool of war. What is unsure is the extent to which these crimes occur. This is due to the lack of empirical data due in part to the underreporting of the practice.

It is without a doubt that male sexual abuse is underreported and this is due to a combination of shame, confusion, guilt, fear and stigma. Men find it very difficult to talk about sexual abuse or being victimized, particularly in societies in which men are discouraged from talking about their emotions. There is confusion about the definition of masculinity and with that of the role of a man. Based on society's definition of masculinity a man should have been able to prevent himself from being attacked—and in dealing with the consequences of the attack—to be able to cope "like a man."

I am able to relate easily to survivors of sexual assault and why they find it difficult to talk about the abuse. As victims living in societies that have a narrow definition of masculinity, men do not have the right words to express themselves. To express oneself, it would be imperative to tap into our emotions and as men, we were never taught how to express our emotions in words. While I have mastered the English language, I find it difficult at times to express how I feel about my abuse unless I use my dialect of Jamaican creole.

Male survivors find it very difficult to report sexual abuse not only because they are unable to find the right words in which to express themselves, they face the danger of not being believed, unable to prove the rape or accused of being a homosexual. It is the fear of not knowing if anyone would believe them that have led many victims to engage in consensual homosexual activity, which may in turn be a criminal offence under the law depending on where the victim lives. The danger of this happening may preclude some victims from reporting the abuse they have suffered.

Researchers Ling and Skjelsbæk, both in 2001, said that most cultures appear to support the claim that an important aspect of conquest involves turning male enemies into feminized subjects.

As Judeo-Christian and Islamic taboos against homoeroticism (including violent homoeroticism) became institutionalized during times of war; acts of sexual abuse as aspects of war became less public, and generally ceased to be part of triumphal spectacles of violence. These continued to be practiced underground, but according to W. J. Webb, in the 2001 publication of *Slaves, Women and Homosexuals*, male victims in the grip of the prevailing taboo found it ever harder to speak of their experiences of male-on-male sexual assault and harder to find those who would listen when they did speak. In his book *Male Rape: Breaking the Silence on the Last Taboo*, Richie J. McMullen summarized the modern state of affairs concerning male-on-male sexual assault and suggested that a victim's reluctance and institutional neglect combines to eliminate the male victim from consideration. As he said, "Many people have difficulty calling a spade a spade."

It is common practice for women to be sexually assaulted by men, and in war this is considered to be an open practice. Sympathy for the female victim varies, depending on the cultural and historical context in which the sexual violence took place. It is a common practice, said B. Allen in *Rape Warfare*, published in 1996, that women who were victimized could no longer return to their communities, as they were viewed as "dishonored" and "impure"; they were either relegated to serving as prostitutes or, in many cases, killed by their own men (often with the complicity of other community women) to salvage the collective "honor" of the group. As W. J. Webb said in 2001 in *Slaves, Women and Homosexuals* there were many instances when women did, indeed, receive care and sympathy from their community, while men and boys were viewed as being able to "take" both sexual and nonsexual abuse, and who similarly risked violating community honor and its "masculinist" code by protesting about their victimization.

In the scant literature on wartime sexual violence against men, one inescapable conclusion is that its consequences are no less far-reaching and traumatic than that experienced by female victims. Sexual violence is still one of the most horrifying weapons of war, a common instrument of terror used against women. Undoubtedly there are a huge number of men who are also victims of these atrocities. If we take a much closer look at wars, male rape is pervasive in many of the world's conflicts.

Fear of society's judgment is a major factor why victims remain silent, and in general, discussion of other forms of sexual torture is looked upon as taboo. As a consequence, victims have kept quiet about their adversities, even among themselves. As with other victims of war, men who were sexually abused suffer from post-traumatic stress, which may include difficulty sleeping, night-sweats, fear, tension, poor concentration, flashbacks, and difficulty functioning sexually. Many also have fluctuating mood states, from depression to aggressive assaults. In a single flashback, a victim is likely to unconsciously identify with the one that sexually abused him. Male victims feel degraded and affected intimately.

For many men, talking about the abuse returns their feelings of self-confidence, especially if they feel that they can contribute to something useful, such as finding the criminal. I have now come to terms with the sexual abuse I have encountered in my life and it was through therapy that I was able to heal. For many men who have been sexually abused, speaking out about the experience helps to free them of the feelings of guilt that perhaps their behavior had provoked the original uncontrolled conduct of their abusers. One of the most important steps in recovery is verbally acknowledging that the abuse was never your fault. This type of traumatic experience men endure during and after sexual abuse is something that hasn't been recorded in history. Depending on how horrific the sexual abuse was on the male such as, the actual forced sexual encounter, beatings on the genitals, and castration can leave psychological scars.

Many of the attitudes, beliefs, and mistaken ideas surrounding rape have been with us for centuries. The myths of rape have been deeply embedded in society, and by looking at the constructions, "the victim asked for it," and "the victim secretly enjoys rape," from a historical perspective, we can better understand how they evolved. In time, our understanding of the evolution of common myths can provide us with a firmer foundation from which to educate people about sexual assault.

A better understanding of myths and attitudes surrounding rape is found enshrined in part in our legal system, which was developed from the English common law system, and which in turn claimed its origins in the Bible. In early recorded history, rape was a ritualistic way by which a wife could be obtained, or "bride capture," as it was termed. This occurred when a man raped a woman and then was able to take her for his wife. Rape was always defined in relation to marriage, and marriage was considered an exchange of property. In Babylonian times, this ritual was considered more civilized and adopted as a societal norm.

There is also the practice of a dowry or bride price, in which a value is placed on the future prospects of a potential bride. In many cultures, the prospective groom paid the prospective bride's family for the privilege of marrying their daughter. Part of the bargain and a potential deal breaker for the marriage was the bride's virginity, which spoke to her purity as being untouched and never having had sexual intercourse, Virginity had to be guaranteed or the price was lowered. Consequently, if a daughter was raped prior to her marriage, it was considered to be a crime against her father, who would then receive less money because his daughter's virginity had been "stolen." The compensation was to allow the father and brothers of the victim to rape the women in the rapist's family and restore their own family's honor. Such reciprocal violence was considered an appropriate vengeance and retribution. In sum, women were considered pieces of property: they were first owned by their fathers and then by their husbands. The "women as property" concept was a first step in the development and institution of slavery.

Hebrew law also contributed to the evolution of some other concepts. In ancient times, cities were surrounded by walls. If a virgin was raped inside the city walls, both she and the rapist were stoned to death. She was considered deserving of death because it was believed that she could have escaped or screamed, if she had been so inclined. If she was raped outside of the city walls, it was believed that she might have screamed for help, but no one would have heard her. In this instance, the victim's father was compensated monetarily, and the victim and rapist, if he was identified, were forced to marry. If the victim was promised to another man, the rapist was stoned to death, and her family received a lower price. If the victim was married, it was considered adultery, and she was considered damaged property; both she and the rapist were stoned to death.

While present-day laws are not nearly as extreme, many of the beliefs and ancient laws underlying modern laws are still prevalent. Consent is the oldest and most frequently used defense against the charge of rape, and rape is the only crime in which the victim is doubted. In other words, when a woman is raped, it is not uncommon that some of the blame and responsibility for the rape is put on her on the theory that she encouraged it. In many cases of boyhood sexual abuse, many victims do not come forward to report their abuser because often they are told that they encouraged the abuse, by their actions, implicit or explicit. This is probably one reason for the incredibly low conviction rate of rapists, for both male and female victims. The criminal justice system reflects the prevailing societal attitude that victims are partially responsible for rape.

Chapter 3

Definition

I never knew that sexual abuse would have had such a lasting impact on my life, even as an adult male. I was naïve to have believed that my perpetrator who raped me at 14 loved me. The abuse has helped to shape my definition of love and trust.

As a definition, sexual abuse is largely based on a geographical location, legal systems, and social science research. In an attempt to be true to the title of the book, I felt that it was important to give my personal definition of sexual abuse. It took me years to understand what I had endured. Oddly enough, I had felt that the man who raped me when I was 14 years old loved me, and while the abuse lasted for about two years; I too felt that I was in love with him. After years of therapy, I now define sexual abuse as someone using sex as a means of power and control. For the purpose of this book, I have decided to take a global approach to defining sexual abuse. I have decided to encompass all aspect of sexual abuse and define it as use of force, threats by anyone in a position of power to make intrusion on another person. In its simplest form, someone in power can simply means a parent or a trusted family member or friend. Sexual abuse can also occur by threatened physical intrusion, by force or under unequal or coercive conditions. Too often we view sexual abuse as only a violent act whereby the victim is held down by force, beaten, tied up, and sometimes killed after the act. While this is true in some instances, there are cases where the individual is seduced and coached over a period of time to engage in sex with their perpetrator.

I will go further and define sexual abuse as forcing any unwanted sexual activity (including oral, anal, or vaginal) by one person on another, either by the use of threat or coercion. Sexual abuse can also be defined as any activity that is believed to be improper or harmful (pornography, touching, foundling, images of nudity on film, electronic media or print). It is important to note that most victims of sexual abuse know their abusers, which leads to unique dynamics surrounding sexual abuse. Most often, sexual abuse only occurs when there is trust; it is this trust that allows the abuser to use coercion as a means to take control over their victim. It is this same trust that prevents a victim from speaking up out of shame or the possibility of not being believed.

For those who are interested in the legal definition of sexual abuse, it is important to note that legal definitions are based on the judicial classification according to geographical locations dictated by social and cultural values. Some legal definition of sexual abuse is used interchangeably with the term sexual assault. Sexual assault may take many forms including attacks such as rape or attempted rape, as well as any unwanted sexual contact or threats. Usually a sexual assault occurs when someone touches any part of another person's body in a sexual way, even through clothes, without that person's consent. Some types of sexual acts which fall under the category of sexual assault include forced sexual intercourse (rape), sodomy (oral or anal sexual acts), child molestation, incest, fondling and attempted rape. Sexual assault in any form is a devastating crime. Assailants can be strangers, acquaintances, friends, or family members. Assailants commit sexual assault by way of violence, threats, coercion, manipulation, pressure or tricks. Whatever the circumstances, no one asks or deserves to be sexually assaulted.

Some countries and cultures that have laws governing sexual assault have a more unbending approach to defining sexual abuse and generally presumes that a person does not consent or is incapable of consenting to sexual conduct if he or she is forced, threatened, and unconscious, drugged, a minor, developmentally disabled, chronically mentally ill, or believe they are undergoing a medical procedure. The majority of legal definitions of sexual abuse all have in common that almost any sexual behavior a person has not consented to that causes that person to feel uncomfortable, frightened, or intimidated is included in the sexual assault category.

Sexual abuse, sexual misconduct, sodomy, lascivious acts, indecent contact, and indecent exposures are all examples of possible sexual assault charges according to legal standards. In both the social science and legal literature, "sexual abuse" and "sexual assault" are used interchangeably.

Defining male sexual abuse is no easy task. It must be noted, however, that male sexual abuse transcends racial, ethnic, cultural, social, class, and religious barriers. Before we get into a discussion about sexual victimization or male sexual abuse, let's be clear about the terms we're using and what they mean. The terms "sexual assault," "sexual violence," "sexual abuse," "molestation," "incest," and "rape" are often used loosely to describe both legal and illegal behaviors that cause victims to feel anything from discomfort to assault and violation.

There is disagreement within both the advocacy community and the criminal-justice system about which is the best, most accurate, and descriptive term to use. Oftentimes we may find that the victims and advocates in our community have preferred terms that will show up in their literature or in their conversations. It can be beneficial to have a conversation with them about why they choose to use certain term(s). Careful definition of terms can increase our mutual understanding regarding shared information and provide an opportunity to clarify viewpoints.

Applicable for this book is a definition of male sexual abuse from the American Psychiatric Association's *Diagnostic and Statistical Manual of Mental Disorders* (Fourth Edition) that states, "Sexual abuse, simply put, is when a person in power or authority uses you or forces you to perform for his or her sexual gratification. Sexual abuse can range from noncontact flashing and use of explicit pictures and language to touching and kissing to digital and penile penetration." Sexual assault, on the other hand, is a broader term than rape and includes various types of unwanted sexual touching or penetration without consent.

Examples of sexual abuse or assault include:

- Someone putting their finger, tongue, mouth, penis or an object in or on your vagina, penis, or anus when you don't want them to

21

- Someone touching, fondling, kissing, or making any unwanted contact with your body
- Someone forcing you to perform oral sex or forcing you to receive oral sex
- Someone forcing you to masturbate, forcing you to masturbate them, or fondling and touching you
- Someone forcing you to look at sexually explicit material or forcing you to pose for sexually explicit pictures
- A doctor, nurse, or other health care professional giving you an unnecessary internal examination or touching your sexual organs in an unprofessional, unwarranted, and inappropriate manner.

There are several factors that contribute to male sexual abuse and that are particularly evidenced in childhood sexual abuse. Research material has suggested that the majority of male sexual abuse is committed by someone the victim knows. In 2008, the New York-based organization, New York City Alliance Against Rape and Sexual Assault, defined sexual abuse and rape as any unwanted sexual act. While traditional literature has focused its attention on stranger rape, the Alliance on its website extends its definition of sexual assault and rape to include "an acquaintance, a family member, or someone the victim knows well and trusts."

*   *   *

The story of Mike (name changed to protect his identity), a twenty-two-year-old resident of New York City who was sexually abused by his father, provides a stark example of the familiarity of abusers with their victims. This is the story of his abuse:

> I am still very scared to tell my story because thinking of it always makes me cry. I made myself believe it never happened. My flashbacks would not go away. My parents were young when they had me. My dad wanted my mom to have an abortion but she said no. My dad would pick me up on weekends to spend time with him. I will never forget that night. I think I was five-years-old, when he told me to open my mouth and close my eyes. I trusted him. He put his penis in my mouth. I knew it was wrong, but at five—years-old, I did not know what to do. Before this happened,

I remember I was what would be called a rambunctious child. After, I became a very quiet and withdrawn child. It did not stop there; it went on for a few more years. I remember him telling me it was our secret and not to tell anybody or he would kill me and my mom.

When I turned seven-years-old, the abuse took another turn. My dad started to do anal on me. I remember him coming into my room and locking the door. At first, it was painful, but after a while my body got use to the pain. I felt worthless. Thinking about this part always hurt. Up to now, at night I still sleep protecting my butt for fear of being hurt.

Years went by and my dad got married. I didn't see him as much. I still had to deal with this issue. I have tried to commit suicide so many times. In school, I hung out mostly with girls so the boys would make fun of me and call me gay. I was tortured by the guys at school every day.

As I got older, I fell into a depression. I would pretend to be perfect, but I was dying inside. Then, when there was a family reunion, my father attended. I had not seen him in a while, and he pretended to be the perfect father. He acted like I was supposed to come and welcome him. He threw a fifteenth birthday [party] for me, and I was okay. I realized he was putting on an act. That night, he came into my room started doing me anally while I was sleeping. For a moment, I thought I was dreaming; the pain felt too real. I woke up and pushed him off. He said why I did that. I said, "Dad this has to stop I can't live like this." He asked, "Stop what?" And he started to choke me. I said, "Go ahead and kill me. Put me out of my fucking misery." He let go of me and left the room.

Now, I am twenty-two-years-old, and I'm trying to put my life together. I had to forgive myself; it has not been an easy process. I have developed same-sex attractions and at times engage in frequent casual sexual encounters. I feel that because of the abuse my life has been destroyed. Up to this day, I know my father is still in denial. I realize I have to forgive myself and move on. Trust me, it hurts, but I have God to help me and support from my loved ones and family here. I can't change my past, but I can shape my future.

Mike still lives with the guilt and shame of the abuse and has spoken openly about the depression he experienced, which resulted from what happened to him. He admits he is trying to come to terms with himself by forgiving himself for believing that the abuse was his fault.

Society's socialization process and culture of masculinity prevent many boys from speaking up about child sexual abuse (CSA). Dun and Williams in their 1998 research paper discussed possible differential effects of CSA for men who are abused by men. They describe the ways in which abuse of men by a man may "model to the victims what is already part of a traditional masculine culture—that the proper role requires physical aggression and dominance, especially in sexual relations." It is also the false definition of masculinity, tainted with the traces of homosexuality that has forced victims of CSA to remain silent. Researchers Banyard, Williams, and Siegel in their 2004 study suggested that most perpetrators of CSA are men; thus, men are more likely to experience abuse by someone of the same sex.

Child sexual assault and rape among young adult males have been identified as a public-health problem in the United States. The problem of child sexual abuse/victimization occurs within high-risk populations such as low-income youths in urban areas. In 2007, researchers Trent, Clum, and Roche suggested that public-health concerns over CSA largely stem from the strong links between CSA victimization and subsequent mental—health problems as well as increased sexual-risk-related outcomes in adolescents. The health complication of CSA has unending ripple effects on society. Not only do we urgently need to do more research, but we need to encourage victims to report their abuse and seek help. Help for sexual abuse victims includes providing them with reporting opportunities to the authorities in order to have their abuser prosecuted, thereby breaking the cycle of abuse, which might prevent the abuser from abusing others. Victims should also be willing to speak with a mental-health professional, who through therapy could help the victim deal with the trauma and the psychological damage he or she has suffered.

While poverty often plays a fundamental role in cases of CSA, homeless and runaway young adults are also at great risk. I am making no attempt to suggest that CSA and sexual abuse among young adults does not occur among other economic groups, but greater incidences seem to be prevalent among low-income youths. In many situations of sexual assault among children and young adults, the perpetrator is usually a caretaker, family member, or a trusted family friend. Several researchers have written that runaway and homeless adolescents often come from physically and sexually abusive family environments. Young adults run away from the safety and security of their homes and become homeless due to neglect by an adult appointed to look after them. Once on their own, these adolescents are exposed to the sexual predatory behaviors of adults and other street youths, violence, or the witnessing violence.

In the Caribbean archipelago, a collection of islands in various stages of social, political, and economical development, by virtue of their shared slavery and colonial history, has similar cultural norms regarding boys and men. In many of these islands, the rate of poverty is very high. In my 2005 publication *The Cries of Men* I pointed out, through my own experience of sexual abuse, the correlation between street boys in Jamaica and sexual abuse. In the book I made several points about poverty and the dynamics surrounding masculinity, education, and the fact that the overwhelming homophobia in the Jamaican culture exhibits intolerance of any hints or understanding of male-on-male sexual abuse. Within the context of Jamaican culture, the narrow definition of masculinity engenders the ease with which young boys are sexually abused. In many households, the absence of fathers makes it ideal for young male victims to not report the abuse out of fear of being called "batty-man," thinking that they are or are seen as less than a man.

The ripple effects of CSA and young adult sexual abuse are the same as adult male sexual abuse. Issues of Sexuality, masculinity, and sexual orientation have been proven to have a significant impact on run away and homeless youths. According to researchers, adolescents with same-sex sexual orientation are more likely to be rejected by caretakers, kicked out of the home, and victimized once on the streets.

An emerging trend in literature on CSA has found that a significant number of boys have been molested within organized sporting activities. An in-depth study, conducted by Mike Hartill in 2008 on boys who were sexually abused, found that the socialization of masculinity with sporting activities has contributed to sexual abuse of male children. Hartill added that the specific issue of sexual violence against males and the male child, specifically within the practice of sports have remained, at best, implicit, but absent from the analysis of masculinity scholars. He posits in his 2008 article "The Sexual Abuse of Boys in Organized Male Sports" that "organized male-sports as a social space that facilitates the sexual abuse of boys. Through promoting a sociological perspective on child abuse rather than an individualized and pathologized approach, I consider how the institutions of childhood, masculinity, and sports fit together and the contribution that sports make to the adult-child relation . . . ."

Research into the relationship between child sexual abuse and organized sporting activities has been limited due to the overpowering tone of masculinity. This was pointed out by Michael Welch 1997 who cited researchers Hall and Hargreaves in his article "Violence Against Women by Professional Football Players: A Gender Analysis of Hypermasculinity, Positional Status, Narcissism, and Entitlement". Welch expressed that within the sociology of sports, the institution of sports is based on a performance-driven structure, which prioritizes and reproduces patriarchal notions of a dominant, heterosexual male. So with this in mind, I am led to conclude that sporting activity, particularly organized male sports, is a social field that plays an active role in the practice and perpetuation of CSA.

Organized sporting activities are usually one medium that is used to reinforce social norms among boys, which have helped to reaffirm gender identities within society. Sporting activities are traditionally used as male bonding and a code for teaching young boys how to be men (touch, strong, independent, team player and how to be physically strong). Several researchers have suggested that boys who are heavily involved in sporting activities are more exposed to the opportunity of being sexually abused.

It is the male code of bonding that too often prevents young male victims from wanting to speak up about the abuse. Boys are sometimes teased, called names and inference are made that they are weak and act like girls if they are not good at sporting activities. As a young boy growing up, I was never good at sporting activities and whenever I was on a sporting team at school, I was the last to be picked. I remember the coach at my high school telling my mother that I was too soft and act like a little girl and suggested that I needed a male figure at home. It is this reliance on a false notion of masculinity and the misogynistic world of male sport, further exacerbated by homophobia, which has instilled fear in the minds of young boys when they are molested within the sporting arena.

Societies' are struggling with and slowly coming to an understanding of the cultural contexts of male sexual abuse. Experts both within the social sciences and medical profession believe that current male-rape statistics vastly under represent the actual number of males who are raped each year. With the advent of popular social networks, and with more media reporting male sexual abuse, shedding light on such a taboo subject, rape-crisis counselors estimate that while only one in fifty raped women report the crime to police, the rates of underreporting among men are even higher. Until the 1980s, most literature discussed this violent crime only in the context of women. The lack of tracking of male sexual crimes against males and the lack of research about the effects of male rape is indicative of the attitudes held by society at large. While it is common knowledge that male sexual abuse does occur, for many it is not an acceptable topic of discussion.

While the media has played a fundamental role in helping to advance the dialog about male sexual abuse, the media should also be blamed for lack of reporting and at those times when they do report, are guilty of using sensational headlines. In recent times, the revelations of sexual abuse perpetrated by Roman Catholic Church pastors and leaders of the Boys Club of America have shone a stark light on this issue. The resulting debate surrounding male sexual abuse has painted perpetrators of male sexual abuse as either clergymen or those involved in organized sporting activity and organized boys' groups. It is important to allow the world to have an understanding of what is going on around us. While journalism in its reporting seeks to remain impartial, taking an objective stance regarding the news and information it publishes, a slant has crept into several reports in which blame is apportioned to one or other group or religion. Only when forced by the scandal of revelations of sexual abuse by its priests and the extent to which leaders in the church had gone to cover up these abuses and faced with criminal prosecution, which would have imposed prison sentences on these leaders for collusion and conspiracy to hide a crime, along with the seizure of assets, that the Catholic Church has come forward.

As a society, we have not fully understood male sexual abuse simply because not much research has been done on the subject. The established feminist movement has dominated the research on sexual abuse and usually views men as perpetrators and not as victims. In the past five years, as the Catholic Church's sexual abuse scandal unfolded, the world gradually began to get an understanding of how sexual abuse affects male victims. More research needs to be done to understand the different dynamics surrounding male sexual abuse. An ecological approach must first be taken in order to fully understand the lasting social effects of male sexual abuse. The pervasive nature of homophobia in culture has made it difficult to approach the subject, which has resulted in a lack of understanding.

There are several contributing factors to male sexual abuse. Literature has suggested that the majority of male sexual abuse was committed by someone known to the victim. Dun and Williams in 1998 in their research discussed different possible effects of CSA for men who are abused by men.

*   *   *

Renaldo (name changed to protect his identity), a Black, thirty-year-old man from New York, described in an interview how difficult it was for him to report or tell anyone about who did what to him.

> It was difficult for me to tell because I was afraid that he might
> have hurt me, if I said anything. I was scared. How do I begin to
> explain what had happened? He was a close family friend. I was
> told I had to respect my elders or those placed in charge over me
> as a child. I feared the repercussions and didn't want to be the

embarrassment of the family, and I didn't know then if I would have been supported or not. I felt like it was my fault. I just didn't know what to do.

As I got older, I felt more embarrassed, and I would be considered weak if I shared that information. It kept me locked up in my mind. I felt isolated from my family and others. I have four younger siblings, and I always felt as though I am an only child because I separated myself from them and played it safe. I refused to go out and take chances. I felt like I was caged in myself, and I could not get out. So I stayed close to home.

I wanted to tell someone, but I was afraid of the outcome. I kept it in, but I noticed the longer I kept it to myself that I was slowly dying inside. When I talked with a counselor, I felt I began to shine from within. I had to stop blaming myself and realized that I didn't do anything wrong. Some adult survivors of sexual abuse struggle for years and then reach a turning point where they decide to commit to healing and improving their lives.

*   *   *

Chapter 4

Types of Sexual Abuse/Assault

Within the past few years, North American researchers have found that one out of six boys is a victim of sexual abuse.

—*Dorais*

As our society begins to learn more about sexual abuse, definitions of this act of violence against a person have continued to expand into a broader range of activities perpetrated by abusers; a single episode of sexual abuse may fall into several categories. While presenting at the 2010 Male Survivors Conference at John Jay College in New York City, I had the privilege of meeting Dr. Mic Hunter, who is a psychologist and one of the top experts on the treatment of male victims of childhood sexual abuse. The list below was compiled from research he did for his book *Abused Boys: The Neglected Victims of Sexual Abuse* and from research I conducted into the many types of sexual abuse. According to Hunter, it is rare for a child to be subjected to only one type of sexual abuse. As more research is conducted and more survivors or victims of sexual abuse talk about their experiences, it becomes clearer that the list below is incomplete. There are expectations that as more people come forward and describe their specific abuse, this list is likely to expand.

Types of child sexual abuse/assault (CSA):

- An adult sexually touching a child
- Incest

- Molestation
- Photographing a child for sexual purposes
- Showing the child pornographic materials or making them available to the child
- Making fun of or ridiculing the child's sexual development, preference, or organs
- An adult exposing his or her genitals to the child for sexual gratification
- Masturbating or having sex or being sexual in front of a child
- Sexualized talk
- Verbal and emotional abuse of a sexual nature
- Forcing overly rigid rules on dress or dressing revealingly
- Date/acquaintance rape
- Marital or spousal rape
- Stranger rape
- Sexual assault
- Multiple assailant / "gang" rape
- Drug-facilitated rape
- Engaging the child in prostitution
- Sexual exploitation
- Sadistic sexual abuse
- Sexual harassment
- Voyeurism

Social science research has usually defined sexual abuse from a female perspective. There is limited academic evidence on male rape, but contemporary data has emerged to show that male rape is a social as well as a public-health problem. Due to the fact that most victims of sexual abuse do not talk about their abuse and some of the few reported victims of sexual abuse identify as homosexuals, not much attention is placed on this taboo topic. Male sexual abuse is a public health issue as there is a direct correlation between male sexual abuse, the transmission of sexually transmitted diseases, alcohol addiction and post-traumatic stress disorder.

The very nature of male rape has been difficult to define. At what point, or when, are male-to-male sexual relations or woman-and-male sex considered rape? Definitions are important for two main reasons: first social and second legal. In 2002 Michelle Davies cited studies making mention of male perpetrated male-on-male rape, which included anal penetration by a penis. Since then, this definition has been expanded to include objects. In the United States, there are more explorations of male rape beyond other males to include female abusers. Within the legal field, sexual assault of men by men has been a topic of debate for years, and definitions of male rape were based on institutionalized male rape, as occurs in prisons, jails, mental institutions, or any facility where men are kept locked away.

Until the 1994 amendment of the Public Order and Criminal Justice Act, which widened the legal definition of rape to include anal penetration with a penis, male rape was not considered significant enough to warrant further examination. The amendment has allowed penalties for abusers of males to be equal to those who abuse female victims. But with language, the definition of male rape becomes more complex. It is the lack of understanding of male sexual abuse and the notion that male sexual abuse is a social problem, linked with the discussions of homosexuality, often reflected in society's thinking and discussion. Other researchers, Walker, Archer and Davies in 2005 put forward that studies have shown that when heterosexual men are raped, for some victims, the rape may be their first experience of homosexual contact. Yet, according to Graham in his research published in 2006, many victims and perpetrators of rape identify themselves as heterosexual, which in turn raises an entirely new subject area and points to differences between "male on male rape" and "homosexual rape."

The term "male on male rape" describes the rape of one man by another man. This however is not true of the term "homosexual rape." While these two terms are valid, it is important when defining male rape to use both in their correct and respective contexts. Male-on-male rape while it can involve two heterosexuals or a heterosexual male and homosexual male or bisexual male and a heterosexual male, should not be confused with homosexual rape, which takes place between homosexual men, as in an act of sexual assault or rape by one homosexual male against another.

Jeffery (name changed to protect his identity), a twenty-seven-year-old Jamaican, gives a candid account of how he was sexually abused by his older cousin. He struggled for years before he could muster the courage to tell anyone his story. Once he was able to talk about his experience, he has been freed of the burden of the secret and has been able to advance his education. He now holds a masters degree in clinical psychology and is using his experience, together with his training, as tools to help other survivors heal.

Seventeen years ago, in 1993, I was ten years old when I was sexually abused by my male cousin. I can still remember the details as if it happened yesterday. After my mother migrated to the United States to obtain the "greener life" for her children, I lived with my Dad. My male cousin Tyvian [name changed for confidentiality] and I were in the house. The person who helped our family with daily chores was in the rear of the house washing, and I was sleeping in my room. I had been feeling sick so I stayed home from school. Tyvian's sexual advances were constant, and each time he seemed to increase his attacks. His actions progressed from grabbing my ass, when I would pass by him, to grabbing at my nipples, to blatantly grabbing me from behind, holding on to me and pressing his dick into my ass.

Around 6:00, later that day, I was lying on my bed when I heard him come into my room and shut the door. Waking up, I saw him standing over me and suddenly he slapped me on my ass, and showed me a condom, telling me what he wanted to do to me and demanding that we use it. I struggled to understand what he was asking me to do. I remembered reading in a biology book, which said that males have penises, so I asked him "how are we going to? We both have the same thing." Immediately, he grabbed my arm, twisted it around my back and held me in a grip which hurt. With his other hand, he ripped off my shorts, and before I could struggle to get out of his grip, he had forced his penis into my ass. The pain was terrible. I felt every tissue in my body tearing, and I lay there helpless while he continued to thrust.

I remember I had looked up and I saw the time, it was thirteen minutes from when he began to when he was finished. Night was quickly approaching, and in the darkened room I lay on my belly reliving in my mind what had just happened. I went over the act in my mind many times, thinking of ways I could have stopped him. Then I started to think, who would believe me? Here I was—the dork, the nerd. My cousin had a different girl every other day; he was the jock—he played soccer, I went to biology class and got good grades; everything I did seemed to be anti-masculine, and he on the other hand had the superior sexual prowess, the male machismo in real life. The thought of telling someone was laughable, and I kept it to my self until seven years later when I went off to university and I discovered psychology and a life time of friends.

It is no longer a secret that rape is used as a tool of war. In the eastern Congo region of Africa, hundreds of thousands of women have been sexually assaulted in the ongoing war. Recent studies have shown that 10 percent of the victims of sexual violence in the region were male. As in many agrarian or rural settings, victims, whether male or female, are often ostracized by their families, communities, and villages. Many are shunned—cast out. For women, they are regarded by the men of the village as damaged and not worthy of marriage. For men, they are seen as weak and less than men. While the six-year conflict in the Western Sudan region of Darfur, as reported by the United Nations, is effectively over, the war has left many shattered lives. It is a common practice for women to be raped during wars, but the act of men raping men in war leaves a more psychological scar on the male victims. Male-on-male rape renders each victim powerless and defenseless, ultimately emasculating them. The guilt and shame, along with the ostracism and attendant isolation of the rapes, have often led the victims into depression, which results in these men committing suicide.

It is crucial to understand homosexual rape within the context of homosexuality. Homosexual rape, which has become a new phenomenon in the social sciences field, involves homosexual men who are sexually assaulted or raped by another homosexual male. Contemporary data regarding homosexual rape suggests that a large number of perpetrators of male rape identify themselves as heterosexual and not as homosexual, bisexual or men having sex with men. But, emerging is a category of men who identify themselves as homosexuals.

In the criminal-justice field, homosexual rape is often confused as a form of hate crime. While there can be some validity in considering homosexual rape a hate crime, incidents of anti-gay violence also include forcible rape, both oral and anal. Attackers frequently use verbal harassment and name-calling during such sexual assault, which gives rise to the action being deemed a hate crime. When homosexual rape results from coercion, the very act seems to imply no homosexuality on the part of the abusers. Harry in his research published in 1992 said that the victim serves, both physically and symbolically, as a "vehicle for the sexual status needs of the offenders in the course of recreational violence."

Within the parameters of domestic violence, as a woman in a typical heterosexual relationship can be sexually assaulted by her male partner, it is also a common occurrence for homosexual men in homosexual relationships to be sexually assaulted by their partners. Because of the stigma attached to homosexuality, too often males in homosexual relationships who are sexually abused do not report their abuse. The same is true for all other forms of sexual abuse; when sex is no longer consensual and is forced, it is sexual assault.

Another area of rampant abuse is that suffered and endured by those young people who through socioeconomic or cultural factors are rendered homeless. Homeless youths who identify themselves as homosexuals and who engage in the sex trade are often victims of homosexual rape. A 2004 research paper "Risk Factors for Sexual Victimization Among Male and Female Homeless and Runaway Youth" by Kimberly Tyler, Les Whitbeck, and others, revealed that "for males, 58 percent reported sexual victimization by strangers, 32 percent by acquaintances, and 12 percent by friends. Although the majority of perpetrators were male, it is interesting to note that 29 percent of all sexual perpetrators of young men were female."

The development and expansion of the Internet has played an increasing role in contributing to homosexual rape. Teenagers and young adults, who are coming to terms with their sexual identity, use online social media networks, such as Facebook, Hi5, and gay chat sites to meet other individuals who are also struggling with their still to be defined sexual identity. Sometimes these encounters turn into sexual aggression and sexual abuse/sexual assault.

With society's misunderstanding of homosexuality, especially since in many societies it is treated as a taboo subject, there is a correlation between male sexual abuse and the acts of a homosexual sexual encounter. The reason behind making such a broad distinction is that homosexuals perpetrate sexual acts of violence among themselves, although homosexual rape is classified when both the victim and the perpetrator identify as homosexual. However, there is no direct correlation between a man who is sexually abused and who later in life identifies as a homosexual.

Dwayne Michael Carter, Jr. more popularly known as the rapper Lil' Wayne, joked openly about being raped at the age of eleven with the encouragement of his surrogate father. He said more candidly on the Jimmy Kimmel show that he lost his virginity at the age of eleven. He noted that the abuse was a traumatic one and that the female who was encouraged to have sex with him was only three years older. Society tends to have a double standard approach towards male victims who are sexually abused by women and more often see the abuse as a rite of passage. Too often in conversations with men about their sexual abuse, I have heard many state explicitly that they would have rather the abuser be a woman as opposed to a man, since mentally it is more acceptable for a woman to force herself on a man than the shame of a man doing it to another man. A young man being able to get aroused by a woman even though forced is seen an act of manhood as opposed to an erect penis when molested by a male. Too often we forget that regardless of the perpetrator, as humans our bodies respond when touched.

Tyler Perry in an interview with Oprah Winfrey on her show in 2010 recalled being beaten and sexually abused by a male and a female relative. He said that the acts made him feel disgusted and pointed out how much it affected his life. After the show aired, Perry and Oprah collaborated to host a two-part series on male sexual abuse.

The concept of boys being sexually abused by women is not a widely accepted social phenomenon. Some argue that it is impossible for a man to be sexually abused by a woman; others view it as sexually exciting. It is very difficult to accept that this notion challenges our beliefs about sex, sexuality, sexual assault, and the constructs surrounding sex. Society teaches us that males are dominant beings, while females are more submissive. Men are supposed to initiate sexual encounters, and a man becoming aroused during a forced sexual encounter with a woman is interpreted as he wanted it.

It is much more difficult for a man or boy to come to terms with the experience that he was sexually abused by a woman. Too often men live in silence and guilt and are unable to fully acknowledge that the abuse occurred. It is difficult to talk about abuse simply because based on society's male code, the male victim would have been expected to enjoy it, and more importantly it is a rite of passage into heterosexual sexual encounters. Men remain silent out of fear of being ridiculed, or shunned by their peers. The ripple effect of males being sexually abused by females has a profound impact on heterosexual relationships and also bring about issues of sexual dysfunctions, such as premature ejaculation, trust issues, and at times the avoidance of intimate relationships.

Research has shown that a man who was victimized by a female perpetrator shares similar effects as the man who was sexually abused by another man. Since I began discussing male sexual abuse, few men have acknowledged that being sexually abused by women have affected them emotional or mentally. Yet, male victims sexually abused by women tend to live for years with the shame, and it is much harder for these men to come forward. Research and literature rarely focus on males sexually abused by women, and as a society, we have done a great injustice to those men who were thus abused. Long-established feminist research has helped to perpetuate the myth that men cannot be sexually abused by woman.

Change will come when there is more acknowledgment and acceptance that men and boys really are sexually abused by women. In the meantime, there is need to begin or advance conversations into examining the cultural and social factors contributing to male sexual abuse by women. Additionally, research is needed in this area, and more men need to feel comfortable talking about their abuse. Lil Wayne's and Tyler Perry's openness about their abuse, prominently indicates an area in social development still in need of examination, because of their celebrity status. This should help make more men comfortable coming out of the shadows to speak of their abuse and begin to achieve healing.

Current literature has noted that there is limited data on male rape and that more needs to be done, not only to expose the silent scourge to male sexuality, but also to understand both sides of the abuse, the abuser and victim. Brownmiller, in 1976 and Taylor Heath and Naffine in 1994 posited in their research that feminist writers have dominated social research and tended to focus on women as victims of male violence. Research into sexual abuse was largely limited by feminists, who focused on men as perpetrators. From a political standpoint and the perspective of a patriarchal society where women were seen as less important than men, it was inconceivable that men could ever be victims of sexual assault. Instead, more attention has been given to female sexual abuse and its ripple effects across families, the community, and society.

*   *   *

One significant area of sexual abuse is that which occurs against children, who are seen as vulnerable, pliant, and to some abusers, as just warm bodies for their sexual gratification. The following story is about Castro, a thirty-three-year-old, born and raised in Sullivan County, New York. He describes his story of his experience with both homelessness and sexual abuse:

> All my life, I searched for love and for someone to understand me. I felt different from others growing up with both parents on crack cocaine and seeing them constantly fighting. I had very low self-esteem. As the only boy in a family with three sisters, I felt I was responsible for them, to protect them, even though I had my own struggles going on inside. When I was younger, looking for love in all the wrong places caused me many problems. Early in my life, I started noticing different things happening and not realizing the effect they were to have on me as I grew older. As a young child, I kept to myself, but during the year when I was eleven-years old, things in my household got out of hand: there was the constant mental abuse and dealing with my parents drug

use. They began to physically abuse my sisters and me; I was beaten for any and everything.

Often, I questioned if God was real, and if so, why didn't he come take me away from all the abuse. I remember some days my sisters and I would come home from school and we would have to lock our selves in our rooms because the house was full of drug addicts. At those times, we couldn't ask our parents to help us with our homework, as they were too busy to attend to us. I remember my clothes being so dirty for school that everyone would always pick on me; I tried to do everything I could to fit in. I would run away from home because things started to get out of hand; I just felt I could do better on the streets. As always, I ended up back home to face the same demons.

Once, when I was thirteen-years old, I was on my way to take some bottles to the store to sell for my parents so they could get money for their drugs. On my way there, I met a man who offered to give me extra bottles, since he had been saving them and didn't want to take them to the store. I took the bottles, and when I returned home I told my parents that the man given me the bottles. Over time he became my [like my] godfather, and my parents saw that he could support their habit. At the time I didn't know how old he was, but I later found out he was forty-five years old. He started to come and pick me up to do things with me that my father never did. He took me to the movies and to plays. I liked to sing, so he bought me lots of music. He supplied me with things that seemed to throw me off track, knowing I didn't have these things growing up. I was open to accepting anything, and as a kid I did. My oldest sister didn't like him. She told my parents she didn't want him around me, but my parents would get mad at her and beat her for being "in grown people's business."

I remember the night he came to pick me up and take me to see a Mickey Mouse show. I was excited, but things changed. I wasn't taken to the show, instead he took advantage of me, he molested me and did things to me I'll never forget. I just laid there so helpless and confused. All I wanted to do was to die; I felt like all this was my fault. I made it back home the next morning, and I was very quiet. My sister knew that man had touched me. She was the only one I could talk to. My underwear was bloody from his attempts to push himself inside me.

I lost my respect for my parents, because they put drugs before me and destroyed my childhood. I started acting out: stealing, and fighting. I ended up going to foster care and in group homes. Eventually, I did seven years in prison.

When I was released from prison, I had no place to go. I refused to go to my parents' home since nothing good came out of living there. To survive, I accepted whatever anyone wanted to offer me in return for sex.

That experience allowed me to realize that I had to change, to better my life, because I couldn't let what happened to me when I was younger destroy my life. I realized that I couldn't change my past, but today I live knowing I can change my actions so that tomorrow would be better.

*   *   *

Child sexual abuse is defined as the abuse of children by adults or by older children or peers who use sex as a tool of domination and control, as in the cases of older boys who force younger boys to undress and then fondle them. While sexual abuse against children are usually committed by familiars, those known to the child and who are seen as in positions of authority, it can also be committed by strangers. Most of this type of abuse is perpetrated by adults or older children entrusted with caretaking roles.

A widespread form of sexual abuse is fondling—an adult stimulating a child's genitals or other erotic area, including the anus, buttocks or penis in boys, or in the case of girls, their vagina. Abuse may include touching nipples or probing with a finger, and in the case of male abusers, with their penises. A touch from an abuser can also come in the form of rubbing or hugs, which seem innocuous, but to the abuser, take on a sexual meaning when the victim is held tighter than normal and the abuser places his or her hands on the lower parts of the victim's body. The adult then rubs his or her body against the child's body for stimulation.

Evidence of the existence of sexual abuse of male children was brought into stark relief with the 2003 publication of the National Bestseller by Khaled Hosseini's *Kite Runner*. Although a fictional narrative, the novel, which was made into a movie, described how in Afghanistan and Pakistan boys were captured by warlords, kept in a harem, made to dance, and then systematically and repeatedly sexually abused by the men when the parties were over, either in the warlord's accommodations or in nearby brothels.

While sexual molestation of a victim of any age is another form of abuse, it usually involves sexual stimulation to the body and genital areas, which sometimes could include either anal or vaginal penetration, or oral sex. Additionally, molestation could occur, though it may seem farfetched, when an adult chooses to photograph a child for his or her sexual gratification. Included under the act of sexual molestation is voyeurism, which is one person's invasion of another person's privacy, either surreptitiously or openly, for sexual gratification.

Rape by a stranger is sexual abuse, whether it is of a male or a female, and is an act of violence: lashing out in anger, and expressing power, domination, and control over another with sex as a tool and a form of attack. While a rape may involve penetration of a person's bodily cavities, such as mouth, vagina, or anus, it does not have to; it can be done with a finger or use of some inanimate object. Sexual assault is the violent physical attack on a victim's genitals, which as a term can cover a wide range of activities and often describes the rape of boys and men.

Victims of any of the above types of sexual abuse or assault often experience similar reactions. The effects of sexual abuse and assault are called Rape Trauma Syndrome.

- Anxiety and depression
- Impaired relationships
- Low self-esteem
- Sexual dysfunction and promiscuity
- Drug addiction

- Sleep disturbances
- Suicidal ideation and behavior
- Anger and fear
- Homosexuality issues
- Masculinity issues
- Problems with sexuality
- Self blame/guilt
- Shame/humiliation

There are few clear signs that a person has been sexually abused and no clear criteria for how many signs should be present to warrant suspicion, in part, because each person handles the experience of their abuse differently. As someone who is mandated by law to report signs of sexual abuse in the children I work with, I have learned what to look for when I suspect a child has been the victim of abuse. Over the years, recalling my experience and observing others, I know the possible signs: when a child's conversation becomes sexual; if the child was known to be vibrant and active, but in a short space of time has become withdrawn and sullen; if the child's eating habits change; and if, in conversation, the child may be given to touching his or her genitals or buttocks area in an unconscious act of protection. Other symptoms of sexual abuse can be manifest in psychosomatic complaints, including stomachaches and headaches.

All sexual-abuse signs must be assessed. No one sign alone is enough evidence to indicate that abuse is taking place, but any clinician, before arriving at conclusion, should try to verify the suspicion of abuse through various means, rather than leave the suspicion unexamined.

In extreme cases of sexual abuse and assault, physical trauma such as redness, rashes, and the bleeding of oral, genital, and or anal areas are indicators. Other signs include:

- Bruises on a person's buttocks, lower abdomen, inner thighs, genitals, and or anal area
- Complaints of pain or itching in genital or anal areas
- Difficulty walking or sitting
- Unusual or offensive body odors
- Difficulty in bladder or bowel control

- Constipation
- Pain or discomfort urinating
- Blood in urine
- Abnormal dilation or a prolapsed anus
- Sexually transmitted diseases in the anus, genitals, or mouth
- Bacterial infections, such as yeast infections
- Frequent sore throats, difficulty swallowing, choking
- Ear infections
- Sudden weight gain or extreme weight loss

*　　*　　*

In the following story, Mark (name changed to protect his identity), a twenty-eight-year old from Philadelphia, was sexually abused by his neighbor's son. He discusses how difficult it was for him to deal with the abuse and come to terms with his own reality.

> I am a successful twenty-eight-year old male, and I was sexually abused. The word "abuse" can seem like a strong word, especially if at the time it didn't seem like it was abuse. At the naïve age of seven years, it was "our little game" that no one was supposed to know about. It was not a regular thing, since the guy was my neighbor's eldest son, and he was about eighteen years old. There was not a lot of time when we were alone, but whenever we were, it occurred. It spanned a few years, and everything seemed okay. I really didn't think much of it—after all, it was "our secret game."

> However, as I got older, particularly when I hit my early twenties and started searching for answers surrounding my sexuality and trying to figure out why am I attracted to men, I started to feel angry and bitter towards the abuser. I started to feel corrupted, and mostly I hated the fact that I was never given the chance at childhood innocence. I felt like it was stolen from me, and I could never know for certain. I cannot say with certainty that I was truly born gay, as I would like to believe.

> I had many sleepless nights, many nightmares, and many tears, but I confided in people I knew I could trust, who had similar

experiences. I started reading about what I could do to help myself. At the time, I did not want to seek professional therapy but I found friends and writing poetry to be very therapeutic. I have definitely come a long way since those questions and sleepless nights. I don't cry about it anymore, and I do not have nightmares or sleepless nights, I think I am well on my way to recovering.

Even though I have come to terms with my abuse and even though I have told them I am gay, I refused to tell my family about the abuse. I don't want them to feel as if they should have known or they have failed me. I don't want them to think that if it had not occurred I would be heterosexual, because in the end it really goes back to the question of never really knowing whether I was born gay or whether I was corrupted. I would like to think I was born gay, but I can never know for sure. I think that if there is scientific proof about whether or not there is a link between male sexual abuse and sexual orientation, then I think my outlook and society's outlook on male sexual abuse would change.

Chapter 5

Myths about Male Sexual Abuse

The myths surrounding male sexual abuse is one of the key contributing factors that prevent male victims of sexual abuse from speaking up or seeking help.

Myths surrounding male sexual assault do not only revolve around homophobia but also around societal perceptions of sexuality. Abusers are usually categorized into three groups, heterosexual, homosexual, or bisexual. Sociological critiques of homophobia have noted that the fear of being gay is based on both social and the unconscious thought processes: homophobes fear acting on their homosexual desires. These social fears are also deeply rooted within cultural and some of society's minority groups. Some cultural groups, especially those within the Caribbean region and those countries that were under colonial rule, mainly some African countries, shun the discussion of sexual abuse. Q. Moore, in the 2007 article wrote, "Our community has an unhealthy understanding of our own sexuality and that goes back to slavery." Religious beliefs are closely woven into cultural values and some religious institutions teach hate and encourage a negative approach into understanding male sexual abuse, and they deliberately draw a line between male sexual abuse and homosexuality which is thought to be a sin and against religious beliefs. Too often the sexual act is confused with the actual act of violating an Individual's space and by using sex as a means of power and control. It is these confusions coupled with cultural, social and religious beliefs that have prevented men from speaking up and allow individuals to understand more about male sexual abuse.

Some of the common myths about sexual assault include:

- Myth Number One—Boys and men can't be victims.

  Reality: This myth, instilled in the early years of childhood and sometimes referred to as the "macho image," declares that males, even young boys, are not supposed to be victims or even vulnerable. We learn very early that males should be able to protect themselves. In truth, boys are children—weaker and more vulnerable than their perpetrators—cannot really fight back. Why? The perpetrator has greater size, strength, knowledge, and authority. All of which are exercised as power from a position of domination, using resources such as money or other bribes, or outright threats—whatever advantage can be taken to use a child for sexual purposes.

- Myth Number Two—Homosexual males perpetuate most sexual abuse on boys

  Reality: Pedophiles who molest boys are not expressing a homosexual orientation any more than pedophiles who molest girls are practicing heterosexual behaviors. While many child molesters have gender and or age preferences, the vast majority of those who seek out boys are not homosexual. They are pedophiles.

- Myth Number Three—If a boy experiences sexual arousal or orgasm from abuse, it indicates he was a willing participant or enjoyed it.

  Reality: In reality, males can respond physically to stimulation (get an erection) even in traumatic or painful sexual situations. Therapists who work with sexual offenders know that one way a perpetrator can maintain secrecy is to label the child's sexual response as an indication of his willingness to participate because he was aroused: "You liked it, you wanted it," they would say. Many survivors feel guilt and shame because they experienced physical arousal while being abused and felt their bodies betrayed them. Physical (and visual or auditory) stimuli are likely to happen in a sexual situation. It does not mean that the child wanted the experience or understood what happened at the time.

• Myth Number four—Boys are less traumatized than girls by the experience of abuse.

Reality: While some studies have found males to be less negatively affected, more studies show that long-term effects are quite damaging for either sex. Males may be more damaged by society's refusal to accept their victimization, and by their own belief that they must "tough it out" in silence.

• Myth Number five—Boys abused by men are, or will become, homosexual.

Reality: While there are different theories about the development of a person's sexual orientation, experts in human sexuality do not believe that premature sexual experiences play a significant role in late adolescent or adult sexual orientation. It is unlikely that someone can make another person a homosexual or heterosexual. Often it's a combination of both biology and the nurturing process that contributes to the development of a person's sexual identity. Sexual orientation is a complex issue and there is no single answer or theory that explains why someone is likely to identify as homosexual, heterosexual or bi-sexual. Whether perpetrated by older males or females, premature sexual experiences of boys or girls are damaged in many ways, including confusion about one's sexual identity and orientation.

Many boys who have been abused by men erroneously believed that something about them sexually attracted the men, and that this may mean they are homosexual or effeminate. Again, this is not true. Pedophiles who are attracted to boys will admit that the lack of body hair and adult sexual features stimulates them sexually. The pedophile's inability to develop and maintain a healthy adult sexual relationship is the problem—not the physical features of a sexually immature boy.

*   *   *

The following story, illustrating the power of one these myth, is from thirty-four-year-old Mustafa (name changed to protect his identity) from Sudan in which Mustafa describes being sexually abused by his great uncle, who insisted that Mustafa penetrated him, an indication that since he was sufficiently aroused with an erection, that he enjoyed the experience. I made a conscious effort to reach out to a wide cross section of men to have them share their story, and I am intrigued to share Mustafa's stories. Of all the men that I have met and who have shared their stories, I never had the opportunity to hear from a survivor from the Muslim world.

> I was just thirteen-years old when my maternal grand-uncle molested me. From an early age, I was intrigued with cars, and he owned a car. My passion for cars was no great secret, and my great-uncle, knowing this reality, invited me for a ride and told me he could teach me how to drive. I felt that this was a great opportunity for me to do something that I really wanted to do. Several times during our ride and at those times when the car was parked, he took out my penis and started to massage it, hoping that I would get an erection. I was shocked by my great uncle's actions, and I was speechless and felt ashamed. My uncle told me that everyone does this, so I should not feel bad about it. I explained that I was unable to gain an erection out of shock. This was not the only incident. Over time, I had to endure other shameful experiences.

> The day following the incident was very traumatic for me, because I knew I could never tell anyone what my great-uncle had done, not only because I was ashamed and embarrassed, but simply because I was unsure if anyone would have believed me. The experience bothered me and affected me in school, in how I interacted, and the trust I had for adults. As a result of the shame I felt over the years, I have not spoken to my mother, brother or any other siblings about the incident.

> Five days after the initial incident when my great-uncle fondled me in the car, he came by my mother's house and asked if she

could allow me to come over to his place to help with a light bulb because he had a bad foot. I could not refuse, otherwise I would have had to give a reason for not wanting to go with him. I agreed and went over knowing that he was going to make me do things I didn't want to do. When I got to the house he came toward me and took my penis out of my pants again and started playing with it, telling me to relax this time. I was still in shock, not having recovered from the previous experience in the car. More than thirty minutes later, almost an hour, my uncle continued to play with my penis until it became erect. Then, he removed his pants and ordered me to put my penis in the back of him.

I carried the guilt and shame locked up inside until I moved to the Netherlands, when I confided in a few of my very close friends. The shocking part of my experience was that I knew of other young boys who were also forced to have sex with him. I suspect that my older brother may also have been forced, and though happily married with a family, we never spoken about our past together. In 2008, my great-uncle died and I was elated and overjoyed that he would never live to harm another child.

*   *   *

Philip's story is of his abuse from his second cousin, and demonstrates how he was unsure if his abuse contributed to his homosexuality. Now living in Amsterdam as a forty-year-old man, he spoke of his sexual abuse by a family member and the emotional abuse he suffered and endured from his family for more than thirteen years.

One afternoon around noon, my grandmother had left for work and my second cousin, my great uncle's son, who was probably around the age of fifteen-years old, was having problems home with his mom and stepdad and he ran away to my grandmothers' house. I remember I was only about four years old at the time, and both of us were home alone. He and I were in the kitchen eating Vienna sausages with curried rice, which my grandmother cooked. I still remember that day very well. When we finished eating there was two sausages left in my plate and I was standing on a chair.

After my cousin finished he went and locked the kitchen door, which everyone did, as no one was home besides us and normally around that time we go and take a midday nap. As I was walking to go to the toilet through the room where he slept, he came up behind me and pulled me into a closet that was next to the wall in the bedroom behind the toilet. Before I could realize what had happened, he had pulled down my pants so fast; he shoved his penis up in me. It hurt, and I can not remember if he was doing it over and over but it was for quite some time. I came out of the closet and went to the bathroom to try and wipe my butt and noticed blood—lots of blood.

Later that day, around 6:00 p.m., my mom came home. In the meantime, the house was full of my other cousins and aunts and uncles. I wondered if I should tell my mom what happened. I knew how my aunts and uncles liked to argue as they did every day on the patio outside. I knew they did not like my mother, so I kept my mouth shut, and I did not tell her anything. I remember the day before I asked her for the translation of a woman's period in English. She slapped me very hard across my face and said that that was not any language for me to use. In fact I had heard my older cousin saying that "he" had that and that he has lots of blood coming from his butt; he showed us, for at that time in 1976, he thought he was a woman.

The experience from that day has left me with many scars and as a result to avoid an argument, I kept the secret from the family. There was always an argument in the house involving my mom, and she would cry constantly; I didn't want to add to her burden.

I was never angry with my cousin for what he did, but later in my life, it became a struggle to determine if I was gay or not; not knowing if it was as a result of the sexual abuse. I still have not accepted the reality that I am gay. As I grew older I tried never to think of that incident. I now live my life the best way I know how, and I am very close to God, for He has never forsaken me.

One thing that came as a result of my sexual abuse was my desire to have sex with men. When I was twenty-years old, I decided to experiment by having sex with men who had the largest penises, so that I could relive my first sexual experience. I became very promiscuous and slept with many different men. I learned more about my body and how much I could be mentally affected. On many occasions I tried to kill myself, but it was as if I was hearing the voice of God telling me that the same strength one has to kill ones self is the same strength one needs to live. The worst part was not so much about the rape; it was that I felt alone, and coming from a very large family with almost no one who seemed to care or show me any love.

Christmases and Easters should be times of togetherness, when families come together, but I was left out of my family's celebration. One Christmas, everyone woke up early to go to church and returned home; there was a present under the tree for everyone and none for me. I ran into my room, as my mom had gone to work, and cried. When I was twenty-three-years old, I told my mom about the abuse. After all these years, my mother has no hatred towards the rest of the family and what had happened to me. In her own way, she taught me forgiveness.

Chapter 6

Society's Views about Male Sexual Abuse

Male victims of sexual abuse comprises of an extremely under-identified, underserved and frequently misunderstood population

2007—Moore and Queshanda stated that one in thirty-three American men is a victim of sexual assault. In 2005, the National Crime Victimization Survey found that 73 percent of sexual assaults were perpetrated by a nonstranger.

2006—Tjaden and Thennes stated that about 3 percent of American men—a total of 2.78 million men—have experienced a rape at some point in their lifetime.

2006—Tjaden and Thennes stated that 71 percent of male victims were first raped before their eighteenth birthday; 16.6 percent were between eighteen and twenty-four years old when they were raped, and 12.3 percent were twenty-five years or older.

2006—RAINN report, although it is estimated that men make up 10 percent of all victims, they are the least likely to report a sexual assault.

2003—National Crime Victimization Study said one in every ten rape victims was male. While there are no reliable annual surveys of sexual assaults on children, the Justice Department has estimated that one of every six victims are under twelve years of age.

2003—The US Department of Justice said that 13 percent, 31,640, of reported rape and sexual assault victims were male.

2001—The international human rights organization, Human Rights Watch in 2001 said that 22 percent of male inmates have been raped at least once during their incarceration; roughly 420,000 prisoners each year.

In academic literature, there is little empirical data for reference when discussing male rape. The majority of victims never seek help. But the figures that are available are from the few men who did report their abuse as a crime and other data are presented from medical professionals: from psychiatrists, medical doctors, and rape-crisis counselors. According to the US Department of Justice 2003 report on estimates from 2002, the most recent statistics, more than 247,000 women and men in the United States have been raped or sexually assaulted. These low numbers are due largely to a feminist approach to researching sexual abuse and gender differences when reporting the rates of rape.

According to the Rape Abuse and Incest National Network (RAINN), a sexual assault occurs every two and a half minutes. Researchers Pino and Meir in their 1999 publication said that preliminary results suggested that men are 1.5 times less likely to report a rape by a male perpetrator to the police than a woman. Other researchers, Finkelhor, Hotaling, Lewis, and Smith in 1990, and MacMillan and others in 1997, in their respective publications suggested that 4 percent to 16 percent of men have been victims of sexual abuse during childhood.

To be able to arrive at some understanding of male sexual abuse, a person needs to become familiar with the terms and concepts that make up the study of society—sociology—what it stands for, and more particularly, its importance in helping to change social perceptions about male sexual abuse.

Toward the end of the nineteenth century and the first half of the twentieth century, sociology was developed as an academic discipline, based on the theoretical writings of Karl Marx, Emile Durkheim, Max Weber, Talcott Parsons, Robert Merton, and James Coleman. As a social science, it encompasses and traditionally focuses on social stratification, social-class structure, social mobility, religion, secularization, law, and deviance. It is social deviance that has led to broadening the scope of sociology and how it is viewed. The discoveries of new sexual deviations and perversions practiced by humans had many unintended effects on extending the scope of sociology. Sociologists realized that sexual deviations and perversions, such as sexual abuse, fundamentally impacted society and the mental health of those living in any given society.

Within the public-health field, it is a known fact that there is a direct correlation between sexual abuse and sexually transmitted diseases (STDs). Male victims of sexual abuse are less prone to talk about their abuse or sexual assault, and as a result, their denial, shame, or reluctance often lead to increases in the spread of STDs. As a separate subject, STDs will be discussed in more detail in later chapters.

From a sociological approach, in public health, the role of social and behavioral factors in health and illness is crucial. Social science has failed to keep abreast of the progress and advancements in public health. In this twenty-first century, there are many unresolved social problems brought forward as baggage from the previous century, including a dearth in sociological and social science research into male sexual abuse. The feminist movement has been successful in developing a methodology, which has sensitized society to their issues of sexual abuse, but this process has not crossed over to extend any sympathy and empathy to male victims of sexual abuse. The development and implementation of sociological theories, which have helped the feminist movement, need to be employed in conducting more research into male sexual abuse, through social surveys, uncomplicated questionnaires, and focus on male victims who do not identify as homosexual or bi-sexual, so as to get a better understanding of the scope of male sexual abuse, and in so doing, determine at least whether or not a sexual-abuse victim is homosexual or whether or not a male sex abuser is homosexual.

As a result of centuries of enculturation, misogyny, and an emphasis on a patriarchal society, misconceptions have emerged about male sexual abuse, as I discussed at length in the previous chapter. In my conversations with people about male sexual abuse, there is an immediate assumption that

I am talking about homosexuality or to a greater extent, advocating for gay rights. One of my greatest challenges when engaging in discussions on male sexual abuse is to assist my listeners in making the distinction that there is no correlation between male sexual abuse and homosexuality. While some sexual abuse may be same sex in act, studies have also shown that women sexually abuse young boys and men. This led me to realize that there was a fundamental problem in the definition of words based on how we are socialized.

My interest in the dynamics of sociology was piqued when I attended community college and later university. I wanted to get a basic understanding of human beings, how we function, why it is that some people are different from others, and why some groups are judged differently by and from others. I knew from an early age that there was a huge difference between genders and more importantly, between sexuality and the sex act. My approach to the subject of sexual abuse as society views it, in this book, is unconventional.

Over the years, sociologists have broadly defined society as people who interact with each other, using a shared value system of morals and culture. The diversity of culture is as disparate as night and day and may include ethnic or racial concepts, gender, or commonly held belief systems, values, and activities. For any given society, its geographic location is likely to have the most meaning of how specific people live, and location usually indicates people who share a common culture in a particular location. For example, people living in a tropical or equatorial climate have a much different culture than those in much colder or temperate climates.

As part of my research, I asked some of my coworkers and random strangers, "What are your views on male sexual abuse." The purpose of this vague question was to allow me to analyze the answers and to try to arrive at a greater and basic understanding of society, through the lens of how a representative sample of ordinary people view male sexual abuse.

A twenty-four-year-old man said, "I believe that this incident is very common and is kept hidden by victims due to the taboo and prejudice, as well as the cultural stress resulting from being a victim of this type of abuse.

I think male sexual abuse occurs as much as female sexual abuse, but fear of shame and isolation by society makes this incident less reportable."

A young woman, who is twenty-five-years old, said that male sexual abuse is a widespread issue that is often overlooked in the field of mental health. Not enough research is conducted, about the age groups and warning signs of victims.

"I feel that male sexual abuse is overlooked and not addressed enough publicly," a twenty-three-year-old young woman said. "It is something that is not taken as seriously as it should, due to gender being stereotyped as strong (masculine) and as if nothing like this would ever occur. It is just as traumatizing and impacting as female sexual abuse, yet the masses do not address, take action, or sympathize much with males who have encountered such occurrence."

But a thirty-year-old woman, who in her response seemed to suggest that she might have thought considerably about this subject, may have done some reading, or pursued some study where this aspect of human sexuality was covered, said that sexual abuse in itself is something terrible to go through and its consequences are long term. However, from a cultural perspective, it could be said that male sexual abuse, because it is less talked about, is definitely devastating. There is shame, feelings of self doubt, and issues with individual sexual orientation—whether there is a thought process due to the abuse or a possible self reasoning for the abuse to have taken place. There is also a feeling of doubt about and how family and friends would look and view the victim henceforth. Long-lasting consequences are unfortunately more common than we care to admit.

"I believe that male sexual abuse is a big problem that has been overlooked. I feel that in our society it is a topic that is not talked about as much as it should be. People need to be more aware of male sexual abuse as it is very prevalent," said a twenty-five-year-old woman.

A thirty-six-year-old man said in response that an abuser should be punished. The abuse destroys the lives of victims and prevents them from having stable, trusting relationships.

"A lot of men and boys hide the reality that they were abused by a male because they think that it is not right for a man to touch another man sexually," said a twenty-one-year-old young man. "It is not talked about in society, because it is not seen as a common occurrence as female sexual abuse."

*　　*　　*

The story of Matthew, a thirty-one-year-old New York City resident, is about his abuse when he was around four or five years old by his uncle. He shared how, as a young gay man, the abuse influenced his sexual addiction.

> [In] my earliest memories of my youth, I remember that as a boy growing up I was always a little skinny, overly feminine [child]. My earliest memory of being molested was by an uncle. I do not remember how it started. I think I was around the age of four or five. It wasn't penetrative sex; it was mostly me giving him oral. At that time I never knew what that was or what I was doing. All I knew then was that his penis was thick, dark, and hard, and he wanted me to put it in my mouth. From there it was experimenting with older cousins. This happened quite frequently until my teenage years. I was never masculine, and I was called the "fem" boy. I was always the one giving oral. At one point, I remember them "putting" the head to my anus just to see how open it would get. They never fully penetrated me as in having all the way sex; they only put the head of their penis at my anal opening.
>
> There was a guy in school, from the seventh grade until the eleventh grade that I messed around with. In public we were always into physical fighting, but behind closed doors, I was giving him oral. Growing up was really hard for me. As far as fitting in, I really was not into sports (football, baseball); I was into cheerleading and I wanted to play the clarinet, but I was told that it was a girl's instrument, so I picked the saxophone. I always had the feeling of "me not going to it but it comes to me." I was able to have guys come on to me. I don't know if you would consider that a gift or a curse. Now, as I have matured [and] enlisted in the army

as a means of proving my masculinity, I have now defined in my adult mind what masculinity means to me. I am a very sexually active gay male. I mostly engage in oral sex as I get off on giving a guy pleasure. I mostly do not think about what happened to me when I was younger. I know that my past has helped to shape the man that I am today, and for all the men in my past who took advantage of me, they all robbed me of my innocence.

*　　*　　*

When I asked the question about sexual abuse, of a thirty-year-old woman, she said that male sexual abuse is a common societal issue which has been underrepresented. Her opinion was that many males (both adults and teens) experience negative behaviors as a result of this tragic, taboo trauma. Parents, law enforcement, and mental-health professionals as a whole should invest more time and effort into preventing other forms of male sexual abuse through education. Male children suffer more because of the added taboo. Many parents ignore the signs. Male victims tend to act out aggressively as a result of the abuse on other members in their family and have an issue with relationships and communication.

A twenty-seven-year-old woman said that the issue of sexual abuse is gaining more attention. If the conversation is about male-on-male sexual abuse, it is not really known as a popular issue. But, in those instances when men are abused by women, some people seem to dismiss it because the common view of the stereotypical male role is that he is expected to be dominant and be strong. Some people may feel that it is the man's fault for letting himself become abused. This is a more common issue, she said, which needs to be talked about more.

"I believe that we need to have more support system[s] put in place to help male victims, and we need to talk more about female perpetrators," she added.

Sexual abuse among men is just as common as among women, said a thirty-one-year-old woman. Since society places restrictions on men, in which many can't or shouldn't express emotions or admit to being sexually abused, many cases of male sexual abuse go unreported.

A thirty-three-year-old woman said, "I believe that male sexual abuse is just as horrible as female sexual abuse. The abuse takes away so much from the individual and it is very difficult to repair the damage done. It may take a lifetime for a victim to recover."

Another woman, who is twenty-four-years old, said that male sexual abuse probably occurs more frequently than is reported due to the stigma and fear that surrounds it. People hear sexual abuse and immediately think about female sexual abuse, and she called for more advocacy and education about the effects of male sexual abuse.

But a thirty-five-year-old man said that in his opinion male sexual abuse is by and large under reported. He believes that it happens more often that many people realize. It happens not only in institutional settings but at times out of a necessity for perpetrators to exhibit control over their victims.

"I believe alcohol and drugs may play a role in male sexual abuse, especially in regards to adult male sexual abuse. It is not uncommon for male victims to be abused by family members and out of fear and shame, refuse to report the crime out of the necessity to protect the family," he added.

Chapter 7

Masculinity and Sexuality

Society's definition of masculinity and sexuality has tainted how men view themselves and as a result has created a false sense of identity and definition of who a man truly is.

I grew up with a misguided definition of what masculinity was all about. At one point in my life, I felt that a man was expected to have a wife, children—at least two or more—and provide for his family; all of which I believed made a man. As a teenager, the definition of a man became more narrowly defined when I felt that a man had to be able to participate in physical sports, since sports made him more of a man, and be able to be detached from his family, which is avoiding any display of feelings or emotions. As I grew into my twenties, I held the view that developed muscles with a rippled chest, penis size more than eight inches, and a high libido were the definition of what it meant to be a man. Masculinity in my mind included several broad definitions that encompassed a man's physical stature.

I was told in no uncertain terms that real men never had sex with men and any man who had desires for another man or who touched a man sexually, forced or not, was deprived for life from what it meant to be a man. My definition of masculinity was defined by my cultural upbringing and from the ethnic group within which I was born. It was inappropriate for a man to cry. A man who did not have three or more children before the age of twenty-five years brought dishonor on his family. Let's not even have a discussion on homosexuality, especially within the context of those of us who live in the African Diaspora. To become or have homosexual desires or tendencies wasn't only a sin and abomination against God; it was a rejection of one's masculinity.

Catherine MacKinnon in 2005 wrote that masculinity is assumed to be uniform and gender neutral, making all men sufficiently equal to one another so that no man can be in a significant position of powerlessness relative to another man. And, Nalavany and Abell in 2004 wrote that social myths associated with the sexual abuse of boys are derived from the methodology of masculinity, that is, how we socially construct machismo. But, MacKinnon noted that men who are sexually assaulted are thereby stripped of their social status as men. They are feminized: made to serve the function and play the role customarily assigned to women and as men's social inferiors. Within social science when discussing the social myths of male sexual assault, Sivakumaran in 2005 used the term "emasculation" to describe what happens to male victim of rape. This is where a male victim has been stripped of his masculinity, which in turn has made the victim weak and effeminate. It is this fear of being perceived as less of a man that has forced male victims to be silent.

These were some of the age-old definitions of masculinity that were drummed into my consciousness from an early age and that instilled fear and contributed in large part to my reluctance about speaking out about my abuse for many years. Additionally, I knew that not only did I have homosexual inclinations, but feeling more comfortable in that skin, made me remain silent. To my family, the community, and society, I was everything that was weak. It was hard enough accepting my sexuality, but it was a more difficult challenge trying to fit in a world that never fully understood me. My homosexual penchants would be used as a justification of the sexual abused I endured, and I would be indirectly blamed for the abuse. I, too, blamed myself as I saw my homosexuality as a curse and a reason why I was abused, but I was powerless to do anything about it. It was the shame and guilt of not wanting to be less than a man or being identified as a homosexual that forced me to remain silent for so many years.

Society has ignored the prevalence of male sexual abuse on the principle that it involves sexual activities between two men, and as the keeper of the morals and culture of a people, it considers any such contact to be indicative of homosexuality, regardless of any elements of coercion or force. The influence of religion as contributing to the rise of homophobia within society, and acting as a bulwark against recognizing the more diverse spectrum of human sexuality, confined male on male sexual abuse in the shadows. The researcher Sivakumaran in 2005 wrote that this amounted to a "taint" on the part of the victim of rape. Finkelhor in 1984 revealed that the majority (84 percent) of those who perpetrate sexual assault are heterosexual males, 83 percent of child molesters are heterosexual, and Groth in 1979 suggested that the remaining 17 percent are bisexual.

*   *   *

The story of David, (name changed to protect his identity) a forty-two-year-old man who lives and works in New York City, spoke in an interview about how he was sexually abused by his uncle. The abuse, he said, so devastated him that he eventually became a drug addict. Following several years struggling with the pain, he was also able to speak of how he developed the strength to overcome and survive.

> I am currently forty-two-years old and a victim of sexual abuse. The abuse occurred at the age of eleven. The person who abused me was my great uncle. It happened one time around the Christmas holidays. My mother, who was a single parent at the time, was struggling to hold onto the house and raise three children on her own. There was no money for Christmas shopping. I was convinced that I had to perform oral sex on him, in exchange for Christmas presents for my brother, sister, and myself. The abuse occurred only once, but it has left a lasting imprint on my life.

> After it occurred, it brought me through a phase of sexual confusion and denial. I became withdrawn from my family, my grades fell, and I remember gaining weight, as a cushion. As I got older, I started to remember what had happened, and used alcohol and drugs to try to forget. It also carried over into my relationships with other males as I got older. I felt "obligated" to have sex with those who asked.

> As an adult, I self-medicated as I saw no escape to talking to anyone about what happened in my past. As a Black man,

therapy was nonexistent within my community and was often frowned on. I did not seek help until I went into Daytop Village, a substance abuse program in 1996 in New York City. I had a very low self-esteem about myself. During my early twenties, I became very promiscuous and used drugs and alcohol with every sexual encounter that I had. Because of the combination, I took a lot of risks with my health. The healing started when I finally accepted the notion that the abuse was not my fault. It is important for society to understand that male sexual abuse does occur, and that when it happens to a child or young man, that the abuse was not their fault. Currently, I am living my life one day at a time and thanking God that I was able to survive and live long enough to tell my story. Daytop was a great help and as I got older, I found out about other support groups and attended meetings and events with other men who have gone through similar situations.

*   *   *

Male-on-male sexual abuse is not confined to heterosexuals preying on other men they think or suspect as being gay or as a tool of power and domination. In homosexual relationships, as in opposite sex heterosexual couples in domestic situations, it is also possible for gay men to be assaulted by their partners. Throughout the Caribbean homosexuality is a crime punishable by long prison sentences. In some countries hard labor is added on, and in some other countries it is punishable by death. Because not much is known about male sexual abuse, it is often difficult for many in some cultures to see the sexual act as dehumanizing and victimizing. Until the laws surrounding homosexuality are defined more clearly within the context of its impact on the cultural dynamics of many societies, victims will continue to be further victimized based on the sexual act of the rape or sexual abuse.

*   *   *

This story of twenty-year-old Edward from Miami, Florida, tells of the abuse he suffered when he was a child at the hands of an older male cousin and recounts how difficult it is to see this cousin again.

I am twenty-years-old and single. I never married, but the desire to get married one day and be in a stable relationship is always on my mind. I was sexually abused more than twenty times as a child growing [up] by an older male cousin. The abuse has impacted the way in which I socialize with the outside world, and it has strained my relationship with both my family and with my friends. The abuse started when I was in the third grade and continued for years. At the time when the abuse started, I felt ashamed and dirty and couldn't muster the courage to tell my mother or any other adult, not only because I was afraid, but for the reality that my cousin told me that no one would believe me, because I was a child.

At the time, he was nine years older than me, and to this day I have only shared this story with about five people out of fear of being judged and not being believed. I can still remember the first time I was sexually abused as if it was just last night. No one was home but me and him. He came in the room where I was and forced me to suck his penis; then he forced me to turn around, and he began to slap my butt and said this won't hurt it will feel good but you can't tell anybody. He then started to have sex with me. After that night I thought I would have to go to the hospital because it hurt so badly and he didn't use any protection. I was torn really, and I just cried for days but no one knew

I see my cousin once every two years. and it hurts me to know that someone would harm a child who could not defend himself. To me, the world in which I was brought up I saw as cruel and at times, unforgiving. Sometimes, when I think back, I still feel that I could have prevented or stopped him from doing what he did to me. As a young man now, I wonder how I could have allowed another man to take advantage of me in such a way. Since this happened, I consider myself to be weak and to a lesser extent less than a man for not protecting myself. I have never sought treatment or professional help, and I doubt if I would ever seek help. What good would it do? I feel as though it is in the past, and the more I think about it, the more I regret things and other people in my life who I feel could have prevented this from happening to me.

Chapter 8

Male Sexual Abuse—AnUnderreported Crime

I never reported my abuse at age 21 because I never felt that anyone would have believed me. When I eventually reported the crime I was told that I didn't have a vagina and that men cannot be raped.

Few male rapes appear in police or other official records. Michelle Davies and Paul Rodgers in 2006 suggested that very few male rape victims report their assaults to the police because they think that they will experience negative treatment, be disbelieved, or be blamed for their assault. Society in general and males in particular have trouble thinking of males as victims. I can relate very easily to the desire of not wanting to report the crime. At the age of 21, I felt that I was a grown man and I should have protected myself from my perpetrator. Like so many other men, I understand why they refuse to report the crime out of being disbelieved, gender role expectations, lack of available treatment, and sexual-identity confusion. In the social context of my island home, Jamaica, I would have been beaten or I could be further victimized if I were to have reported the sexual act, or sentenced to prison for up to ten years hard labor.

As victims, most of those who were sexually assaulted choose to remain silent out of fear of society's reaction to them. It is destructive for male victims to remain silent about their assault. F. Grossman in an article, "Male rape victims need to speak out" published in *The Boston Globe* in 2002, said that boys and men who have been sexually victimized are silenced more than women by strong cultural views that "real men" don't and shouldn't become victims. What needs to be done is to let male victims understand that they should not allow society to further victimize them. Grossman added that victims should be aware that it is not their Shame, but rather, it is the shame of the perpetrators and of the culture that allows such things to happen with such frequency.

Research has proven that for years men have remained silent, trapped by shame resulting from two main social phenomena: the false definition of masculinity and homophobia placed together with social myths. Society has neglected male sexual abuse on the principle that it involves sexual activities between two men and considers any such contact indicative of homosexuality, regardless of coercion or force. Given the prevalence of homophobia within society, according to a 2005 article "Male/Male Rape and the Taint of Homosexuality" by Sandesh Sivakumaran, published in *Human Rights Quarterly*, this amounts to a "taint" on the part of the victim of rape. The vast majority of those who perpetrate sexual assault are heterosexual males, said D. Finkelhor, in 1984 in "Sexual Abuse in Male Children and Adolescents: Indicators, Effects, and Treatments," published in *Adolescence*. Eighty-four percent of those who perpetrate sexual abuse are heterosexual men; 83 percent of child molesters are heterosexual; and according to A. N. Groth, who wrote in 1979, the remaining 17 percent are bisexual. It is also possible for gay men to be assaulted by their partners.

Heterosexual masculinity has several broad definitions, which may encompass physical build. Masculinity can be assumed to be uniformed and gender neutral, making all men sufficiently equal to one another so that no man can be in a significant position of domination or powerlessness relative to another man. Within social science when discussing the social myths of male sexual assault, "emasculation," as previously discussed, is frequently used to describe the male rape victim. It is this fear of being perceived as less of a man that has silenced many male victims.

The social myths surrounding male sexual assault revolve not only around homophobia but also societal perceptions of sexuality. R. Graham in a 2006 article said that perpetrators are usually categorized into three groups, either heterosexual, or homosexual or bisexual. Sociological critiques of homophobia have noted that the fear of being gay is based on both social and unconscious thought processes: the homophobe is afraid to act on homosexual thoughts or desires. These social fears are also deeply rooted within cultural and minority groups. Some cultural groups refuse any discussion of sexual abuse, which is a challenge for communities of color to come together and talk. As Q. Moore wrote in a 2007 newspaper article, the black community has an unhealthy understanding of its own sexuality and that goes back to slavery.

Little is known about the myths concerning male victims, but research has identified the following myths: (a) being raped by a male attacker is synonymous with the loss of masculinity; (b) a man who is sexually assaulted by another male is often gay; (c) a man cannot be forced into having sex against their will; (d) men compared to women are less affected by sexual assault than women; (e) most men are incapable of functioning sexually unless they are aroused.

Social bias has been foisted onto the medical profession, which has contributed to the victimization of those men who were sexually abused. Based on the limited conversation that I have had with mental health personnel, they generally have a significantly more sympathetic view of rape victims as compared with laypersons. Some mental health personnel have suggested that they find it very difficult to engage male clients in conversation about sexual abuse. Counseling professionals, Kassing and Prieto said in 2009, are likely to develop blaming attitudes or make myth-based judgments concerning victims of sexual assault. Based on a study conducted among counselors-in-training at accredited counseling institutions, Kassing and Prieto also found that professional, male, mental-health workers tended to blame the victims. One possible way to correct the inequities in training is to include male and female sexual assault in curricula or training manuals.

The sexual abuse scandal that shook the Roman Catholic Church has attracted much public awareness about the issue of male sexual abuse. The widespread media attention has forced many to take a more in-depth look at male sexual abuse and its effects on society. In the spring of 2002, many adult men courageously disclosed childhood sexual abuse by Church priests. Their story of the devastating repercussions of childhood sexual abuse has earned them nationwide attention. Male sexual abuse has a profound impact on the victim both physically and psychologically. Male rape is often portrayed in the literature as at least as harmful as and possibly more harmful than the rape of women, said R. Graham, in a 2006 article.

Phelan in the 2007 article suggested that most male victims often hide memories of sexual abuse, believing they can master it without ever revealing what happened. Sexual assault is often emotionally devastating to men. I can easily relate to these men, as for years I found it very difficult to engage my therapist in conversation about the abuse and I would often not discuss the abuse with close friends. Contemporary research suggest that men are likely to experience vulnerability, depression, suicidal thoughts, sleep disturbance, social isolation, sexual dysfunction, and confusion about their sexual orientation if the abuser was male. There were times in my past where I questioned my own sexuality and felt that my sexuality identity was attributed to my sexual abuse.

In my first book *The Cries of Men*, I made reference that some major symptom of sexual abuse is manifested in many forms of post traumatic stress disorder (PTSD). Another group of researchers, Fredric in 1986, Goodwin in 1985, and Lindberg and Distad in 1985 suggested that types of PTSD symptoms may include, flashbacks, nightmares, numbing of some effects, and a sense of estrangement, sleep problems, both immediate and even long term. In her 2004 book *No Secrets No Lies*, Robin D. Stone outlined David Finkelhor's research on the four major ways in which sexual abuse causes lifelong problems for survivors:

- Stigmatization, guilt, shame, and self blame, which could lead survivors to feel bad and hurt themselves and others.
- Powerlessness and the inability to stop the abuse could lead to passivity, lashing out, or controlling behavior.
- Betrayal, loss of trust, and grief over loss of the relationship, especially when the abuser is related could lead to difficulty trusting others.
- Traumatic sexualization, distress, confusion, and painful inappropriate sexual experience; could lead to obsessions or fear about sex.

Men are more likely to react with anger as a result of sexual assault. Due to silence, those around the victim may be unaware of the reasons why they have behavioral problems, such as anger which may lead to the victim harming someone and ending up in prison, where he is likely to be victimized. Frazier and Schauben wrote in 1994 that men were more likely to react with anger immediately after rape because anger is a "masculine" way to deal with trauma.

Male sexual abuse does not only affect the men who are victims, it has a direct impact on their families as well. If the families are not aware that one of their own was victimized, they are likely react negatively, by denying or ostracizing the victim, which is likely to lead to greater complications for the victim.

After a rape experience, most victims feel an increased sense of vulnerability. Mezey and King in 1989 suggested that some victims become overly concerned with taking safety precautions. Research has suggested that male victims may have negative attitudes towards homosexual men, including committing hate crimes. As Walker, Archer and Davis wrote in 2005, some of the stress that is related to rape is related to the horror of appearing gay or not masculine. But, as McMullen wrote in 1990, it is not unusual for heterosexual victims to seek out homosexual contact after rape or, in contrast, manifest irrational loathing or hatred of all gay men.

Sexual dysfunction is a key element of male rape. Both homosexual and heterosexual victims find it challenging to have well-committed, functional, sexual relationships. Some victims become abusive toward their partners. I have had the opportunity of speaking to a large number of men who are victims of sexual abuse and we all acknowledge that we had some form of sexual dysfunction that many of us identified as addictions. Several men reported changes in their sexual behavior after the assault. Some became promiscuous, while others refused to have sexual relations with either men or women for a considerable time after the assault. Walker, Archer, and Davies, 2005 said that male victims of sexual abuse often experience sexual problems including erectile failure and lack of libido.

Out of fear, most men never report sexual abuse, and the health risks of not reporting such crimes are endless. Additionally, victims of sexual abuse develop mental-health problems, which are sometimes, manifest in an increase in risky sexual behavior. Abused boys are more likely to have intercourse earlier, more sexual partners than their peers, and increased substance abuse. These behaviors put them at risk for acquiring sexually transmitted infections (STIs), which according to researchers Trent, Clum and Roche in 2007, becomes a public health concern because the spread of sexually transmitted diseases have profound ripple effects on society. Rectal and anal tearing and abrasions from the sexual abuse can put victims at risk for bacterial infections.

Exposure to other sexually transmitted diseases and potential HIV exposure can have a profound ripple effect on society if left undetected and untreated. One ripple effect on society arising from a sexually abused heterosexual male within the prevailing social and cultural norms is to place women at higher risk for infections. This is because power dynamics are employed when negotiating safe sex. As a result, research shows that there is a sharp increase in the number of Black women who have become infected with HIV. Many men, in an attempt to disassociate themselves from the taint of homosexuality, may assume a hyper-masculine type of behavior. For male sexual abuse victims, while the act in itself is traumatic, many try to affirm their masculinity by impregnating as many women as they can.

Along with compensating for a damaged masculinity, many victims of sexual abuse turn to substance and alcohol to numb the pain in their psyches or to achieve a false bravado as a coping mechanism. This becomes a further public-health concern as this behavior has a direct impact on both the immediate family and the wider society. Many men reported, according to researchers Walker, Archer, and Davies, indulging in self-destructive behaviors as a consequence of the abuse, such as self-harming, suicidal ideation or attempts, and alcohol, drugs, tobacco, or food abuse. While most literature has made a direct link to sexual abuse of women and substance abuse and alcoholism, data concerning male victims does not exist.

*   *   *

The following story is of twenty-six-year-old K. S. from Kingston, Jamaica, who at age five was sexually abused by his older cousin. He talks about how the abuse impacted his life and changed his views of the world.

The abuse occurred when I was only five-years-old by my older cousin. He was about eighteen-years-old at the time. The abuse lasted while I was living with my grandmother in the countryside. I can't really remember how long, but I knew it occurred for about two to three years until my father came and took me to live with him.

There weren't many coping mechanisms. Oh lord, where do I begin? I wouldn't say I coped. I was young, and I didn't know right from wrong. It messed me up big time; I wonder, if it [hadn't] happened, would I have been better man? My coping mechanism was music, and my favorite artist is Christina Aguilera. [Her most important music for me was her] *Stripped* album. This album motivated me beyond my wildest dreams. I thank God for it. It helped me out when I was going through my suicidal phase. The tracks that speak to me the most, and that reflect my pain are "Beautiful," "Soar," "The Voice Within," "Keep on Singing my Song," "Fighter," "Loving Me for Me," "Underappreciated," and "I'm OK." This album was released at the right time to save me from myself. I did not seek help. There are many reasons why I didn't seek help: because of the guilt and shame [and] I was young. I need therapy now. I am extremely depressed; it goes and comes. I need to be happy when I am young and not when I am old.

It affected me deeply. All my life I [have been] in turmoil. I know I was different;, the way I talk and my feminine actions. Through primary school, I was teased. I was preyed upon by young boys, who constantly teased me. It continued through my high-school days. I remember this one time I was teased to the point that I literally cried in my class while all my other peers looked on. I will never forget that day; the memory still lingers like it happened just a while ago. I remember when I first got a job, and within a few months, I was suspected of being a homosexual. I overheard my fellow coworkers, mainly the men, plotting to beat me up and my friend, who also worked where I was working; at the time I was so scared.

I now realize that the molestation is still affecting me now as a grown man. At the age of twelve . . . I realized I ha[d] developed

Obsessive Compulsive Disorder (OCD). At the age of seventeen, I was very suicidal. I didn't have anyone to talk to. Now, in my life when I should be moving on, I am very insecure. I am never happy, and even [when I am], it never lasts for long. I want to feel how it feels to be in a relationship, but somehow, something keeps pulling me back. I can't even explain it myself. I don't even have a father-son relationship with my dad. I started to shut him out of my life during my adolescence, because when and if he finds out I am gay it would be easy for him to cope because we hadn't had a good relationship.

Some days when I look at his face I can see he his very unhappy because I wasn't giving him [any] attention. If only he knew what I was going through; better yet, if he finds out who I really am, I would be a dead man—sad but it's true. I have shamed him. Writing this is so painful, especially on my father's behalf.

To be honest, I am not coping. I thought by the age of twenty five, everything would be over with all these insecurities and I would stop living in fear of my life, but I was wrong—it's never over. I thought I would be confident and [would]n't care what anybody says about me. My mind is in fear at the moment; I don't know what tomorrow will bring, especially in Jamaica where gays are living in fear. I don't see myself living a lie just to fit in, but in the end, the truth always comes out. Right now, I want to move out of my parent's house, but I can't because of fear, fear I would be targeted by thugs. The number-one stigma that is attached to single guys living on their own in Jamaica is that they are gay. I am afraid that I will be beaten or even murdered. That's why I want to migrate to the USA, where I can be myself. I know it won't stop there but at least [would be] a start.

*   *   *

Society's image of masculinity has been culturally entrenched with claims that men are always strong, invincible, brave, and in control. Prevailing research has contradicted these stereotypes. There are no criteria for male sexual assault. Men of all ages, class, color, physical size, strength, personalities, economic background, and sexual orientation can be victims of sexual assault. Males are victimized as both children and adults, in their homes and, most prevalent, within institutional settings. A majority of literature has focused on stranger rape, that does not, however reflect of the majority of research conducted on male rape. The focus on physical harm in rape means that the key issues such as consent to sexual intercourse remain neglected in male rape, said the researcher Graham, because evidence of physical force is often erroneously equated implicitly with victims nonconsent. Graham said that the limited scope of research done on male sexual abuse suggests that male victims are neglected, and men in general do not appear to worry about their personal safety regarding sexual assault.

Although relatively limited, emerging research is classifying male sexual assault as a growing health crisis. The feminist movement must take some partial responsibility for the neglect of male sexual abuse. The focus over the years has been on the male as the perpetrator and aggressor in male-on-female sexual assaults. Seeing themselves collectively as victims of a patriarchal system, the feminists' focus on demolishing the power dynamics of male cultural and social dominance, the women's movement has not exhibited any need to take up the plight of men as victims. The topic of male-on-male rape is well within the scope of the feminist movement, because the dynamics are identical, as the researcher Sivakumaran wrote, that notions of power, dominance, and gender, all of which play a key role in feminist analysis of male/female rape also feature heavily in an analysis of male/male rape.

The Catholic Church scandal has brought to light the issues and ripple effects of male sexual abuse. More needs to be done to legitimize the cause of male sexual abuse survivors in an attempt to seek more help for victims and allow those victimized to speak up about the abuse. Academic literature aims to legitimize male sexual abuse status as an emerging social problem. Although it is an emerging issue, Graham wrote that it seems safe to assume that it is better understood and more accepting than it was forty years ago.

While blame can be placed all around, one must acknowledge that though the research is slow moving, vast changes have been made in the understanding of male rape. Graham added that society's acknowledgement of adult male, sexual assault in the community is likely to have a corresponding impact on the interpretation of the phenomenon. Society has a much greater role in eradicating social and cultural norms about the myths of male rape. It is the power dynamics of rape coupled with gender identity and the false definition of masculinity that have kept male victims of male sexual abuse silent.

The social-science community should seek to ensure that data on male sexual abuse be compiled, despite victims' unwillingness to report the crime, which contributes to hampering further research. Additionally, more creative ways need to be identified to involve men in the cause of preventing male sexual assault. It is essential, Graham wrote, that those discussing male rape do not repeat mistakes that have already been made by feminists doing research on sexual assault but to learn from them.

A significant shift needs to be made in how male medical personnel deal with male victims. The myths that permeate the medical profession about male rape need to be abolished. Kassing and Prieto in 2009 advocated that counselors, educators, and supervisors need to pay special attention to the learning needs of their male trainees in relation to issues of sexual assault. Until the social norms and cultural values surrounding masculinity and homosexuality are changed, the silence of male victims will remain an unresolved issue.

Chapter 9

Conversations

Self-esteem comes from being able to define the world in your own terms and refusing to abide by the judgments of others.

—Oprah Winfrey

To be able to fully understand the phenomena of male sexual abuse, as others have been affected, I decided to have conversations with some of my closest friends and family members. I asked them how they felt when they found out that I was sexually abused. I also spoke with some of the men I knew who were sexually abused as boys about their personal perception about male sexual abuse and their reasons for not reporting the abuse or seeking help.

These conversations were difficult, as I'd never had it with my friends before; many didn't know I was the victim of sexual abuse. I knew that my friends and family supported the work I was doing, and I knew they loved me. When I think back to one person who is closest to me, if I had ever fallen in love with any woman or wanted to spend the rest of my life with a woman it would be a female friend I had developed a relationship with in high school. She has always been one of my biggest supporters; she will always be there. When she migrated to Canada, I was one her first friends to visit. I realized that we never sat down and had a heart to heart conversation about how she felt about sexual abuse, how she felt when I told her that I was sexually abused, and why she is so supportive of me.

To protect her identity, she has been given the name Nadia.

I felt SORRY! I didn't understand it at first, but I knew you probably had absolutely no control. I am sorry that I could not have done anything different to prevent it from happening.

Yeah, I'll be honest, at first I wondered why, I wondered how, I had lots of questions. But I got to know you very well, I loved you as a real great friend from high school, and I had profound respect for you. And after you told me that you were abused, I began to have a deeper respect for you and our relationship.

Not to mention after you went through all that, you came out of your shell, and you told us as friends who you were and I RESPECTED you for that.

You came clean, you spoke the truth, and you accepted who you were and then you wrote your book and began your foundation after accepting the fact that you needed to be healed, then you had a quest to help others! I just grew to accept, love, and respect you over the years.

It wasn't that I was searching for reassurance or acceptance, it just made me question what my life would be like if I had said something to someone or confided in a friend. Did I have to live a life filled with shame and guilt for so many years? I know for sure that happiness comes only from within, and I have no regrets for the life that I have lived. I am stronger for what I did and I admire the fact that I am loved by a true friend.

I believe that everything in life happens for a profound reason, and God has a reason for introducing people into our lives. There was a friend of mine I met when he was attending college in his junior year. After he completed college he moved to New York and we developed a reciprocal sexual friendship. It was as though we knew each other and he was very accepting of my past and understanding of my abuse. I knew there was something that we had in common but we just never had a conversation about his past.

I will call him Steven. Steven bought my book, and he has told other friends about my work and my foundation. I have asked him on several occasions if he knew anyone who was sexually abused and if he could introduce them to me and have them share their story. We have also had our share of arguments but I admire his support over the years. Recently he said, "I felt like: Wow, dat's crazy. The sexual abuse part, like I told you a few years back, I can basically relate to cause I was molested when I was younger."

I said to him, "I don't remember you telling me that you were sexually abused. Look at all this time I asked you if you knew anyone who was sexually abused, and you never told me that you were sexually abused. If you had said something I would never have forgotten."

"Dennis, back when we first met I did share a little bit of it, and I told you I didn't want to go deep into or talk much of it because that's like a place of anger for me."

"All right. Have you ever gotten help?" I asked.

"No, just self-help, I guess. I mean, I didn't get help, 'cause I subdue the feeling, emotions and experience deep in my memory, 'cause I now been grown, now I wouldn't let that happen."

This conversation is so typical of the many conversations that I have had with friends or men I have met. It surprises me when people share their stories with me. It is also odd that so many of my friends have openly acknowledged that they were sexually abused when they were children or as adolescents. Few of my friends have actually sought professional help or even think that they need help. As I have used alcohol and sex as means to cope with some of my emotional problems, so too, I have recognized in some of my friends. There are a few who engage in substance abuse. I support their fight, and I try not to put myself in a position from which I would judge them.

One of the closest people in my life, one of the few men who have seen me at my lowest and has watched me abuse my body, is the one of two people who have loved me unconditionally, supported me in all of my endeavors, and held me when I had no family to support me. There are very few people in my life that I trust, and he is one of them. If he were to ever betray the trust that I have in him, I would be forced to question my own existence. We have had several conversations in the past about my abuse, my addiction, and my lack of trust for family and those who come into my life. I finally had an opportunity, when I decided to write this chapter, to have a conversation with him about how he felt when I told him that I was sexually abused.

> When you initially said it, I was skeptical, but as you went further into the story, giving details of what happened, I understood the harsh reality. I was also upset not only for what you had to endure, especially when you gave such vivid details, but also the fact that you were so trusting of people. It gave me a jolt in more ways than one. I realized then that, instead of being upset that I led a sheltered life, I should be grateful that I was never in harm's way like that, especially since I tend to be trusting of people. I think it was at that point that I decided to keep people at a distance and don't allow myself to become a victim.

I recently opened up to a mutual friend, who I shall call Kendal. I have always admired him for his style and sense of fashion. We met online and we have developed a special bond over a period of time. We have not had an opportunity to hang out in the city or grab a movie, even though we have set up several dates, but it just never materialized. He recently purchased my book, and though he felt that the information was graphic at times, he commended me for what I was doing. He inquired after reaching half-way through the book, why I didn't say something to him earlier, and he also wanted to know how I dealt with the abuse.

> I had no idea you were raped when you were twenty one. As far as knowing that you were sexually abused, I felt sympathetic to the situation. I can't begin to imagine what that feels like. I know of people who have been sexually abused, and it is something that lingers; it takes a toll on them every now and then. My therapist was sexually abused as a child, and he told me that the majority of gay men he knows have been abused.

I decided to make the conversation more personal by asking one of my cousins, who is fond of me. He and I have developed a very close bond.

He is one of the few family members who has openly embraced my sexuality and has supported my cause. I sometimes marvel at his love and admiration for me.

He said, "At first, I wasn't sure what to think! But then I was, like, are you serious? Why my family? Then I was questioning, why you chose the same sex that did that to you?"

My younger sister, who at times I consider my own child, was thrown when she found out that I was sexually abused. Like most of my other family members, she woke up to the news in the media with my face on the cover of the *Jamaican Observer*. Members of my church back home were not only outraged and spoke negatively about my candidness, they shunned my family. Rather than being supportive, I was told that some members of the church told my family that there were sorry that I spoke about the abuse so publicly. Their sympathy was never for me the victim and the survivor; it was the "shame" that I had brought down on my family that they were concerned with. My sister is now nineteen years old, and this was her response to my question:

> Okay, on a sibling's point of view I was in shock and in denial. Being young at the time and naive about male sexual abuse and homosexuality, I was caught up in society's view and discrimination on the issue. It's like observing male homosexuals through the media and from other persons—you hear it, but you don't really listen and understand what it really entails and the causes and effects it has on people until you truly know someone who is in the position. I personally felt hurt, confused, and angry, then in school we had essays to write on certain topics and mine was always about gays and through that I learnt a lot. Overall, I think rape is a vicious act whether male or female.

Some of these men whose stories I present I have never known in my life, others I met in passing, but we all had something in common—a desire to survive and heal. Others' stories were all unique, but we all had varying reasons for not telling our story or reporting the abuse. The men who continued to inspire me along this journey of change range between the ages of twenty two and sixty-seven years old.

We all agreed that before the abuse occurred, none of us had a clue what male sexual abuse was about. The men who took advantage of us were either close family friends or family members, who we trusted. It is this trust that gave them the power and control over us. It is the trust that allowed these men to feel safe and secure that we would never talk about what they were doing to us, and we would have kept that secret locked up inside of us, out of fear. I truly marvel at how comfortable these men felt, telling me their stories, knowing that we had not developed a bond. The one thing that has brought us together is the reality that we survived and we all wanted to bring about change.

None of the men with whom I spoke felt that they deserved the abuse, yet we all believed that we all played a role or contributed to the abuse. We all felt that there must have been something about us that attracted these men to us or we showed signs that we were vulnerable. Some of us may never get that question answered, simply because we never had the opportunity to have those conversations with our abusers, yet alone felt the courage to confront them. My reason for remaining silent all these years had more to do with fear and shame. Fear that no one would believe me; fear that I would be told that I am a liar or that I must have wanted it. It was also the fear of having my family abandon me because of the sexual act and having me believe that I was a homosexual. Back then, I wasn't prepared to accept the skin I was born in or acknowledge that my sexuality had less to do with my abuse and more to do with my biological makeup.

The youngest of us was raped by his father. Who would have known that a father, a man who had given life to his child would rob his child not only of his innocence but the desire to live?

This victim said, "I didn't want to believe that the man who raped me was my father. I wanted to convince myself that it was a dream. The fear of telling someone and not having that person believe me, coupled with shame, prevented me from speaking up."

I, too, lived a lie—the life we lived was like a dream. Until I was twenty-years-old, the fourteen-year-old boy who was raped by the next door neighbor was trapped inside of me, and I had to set him free. I grew up not knowing my father and yearned for a male figure in my life, not to replace my father but to teach me how to be a man. While some male victims within the minority community knew our fathers, for many, they were absent in our lives. We were forced to question the relationship between the absence of our fathers and the molestation and rape by men we trusted. If our fathers were present in our lives, would it have deterred the men from taking advantage of us?

As children growing up, none of us felt comfortable talking to our peers, as children often can be cruel; the conversation surrounding male sexual abuse was a very difficult one to have and being judged by our peers was not an option. For many, fear often comes from not knowing how those around us would react or if they fully understand what we experienced. We all agreed that it's never comfortable having the conversation, it's as though we never wanted to face reality and just wanted to put it all behind us. As one person said, "I don't want to face reality. It's as if I have locked the memories away and the fear of going back is scary. Going back isn't easy, because it makes me emotional, feeling as if I am too weak and less than a man."

Most of us agreed that we all lived a lie; we created an illusion of the life we so desperately wanted to live. Too often, we would play dress up to mask the pain that we were feeling on the inside, simply because we did not want to make ourselves feel vulnerable or weak on the outside.

* * *

In his story, forty-eight-year-old Garfield from Amsterdam, in The Netherlands, describes how at fourteen-years-old he was raped by two men. The first time it happened, he was cruising the streets when he met one guy who took him to his house. While there, another man came in, and they both raped him. Garfield related that, during his teenage years, he was often sexually abused by his rugby coach.

> I consider this episode of my life as an accident. When I was fourteen, I was very curious about sexual activity, and I was looking for new experiments. One day, I was cruised by a man in the street. He proposed to take me to his house to have sex, and when I got there; his boyfriend was in the house. When I realized that we would not be alone, I began to feel uncomfortable with

the situation and decided that I wanted to go home. Both men refused to let me go, and they used their adult strength to force me to stay and they both raped me very violently.

After that episode, I've kept my sexual life on as normal a basis as possible and never had mental problems about that. The only legacy I could talk about this story is that I was unable to be a bottom with my sexual partners until the age of thirty four, [when] I met a man I fell deeply in love with. And I think the will to please him was stronger than the fear of being bottom again. And until now, I still have difficulty being a bottom on a regular basis. I have been in a stable relationship for more than twenty-four years, and it is going strong. I had the opportunity to tell my partner about the abuse, which allowed me to open myself more and be more comfortable in my relationship.

While there are men who may link their sexual abuse to their sexual identity, I am unable to do that. I am not traumatized by the abuse anymore, and I have come to terms with my past and I speak very freely about the abuse. Some men take many years to tell someone that they were sexually abused. Others choose to never tell. As a teenager, I never wanted sympathy and had no desire to make it seem as though I had mental issues. I yearned for the independence to be a man. I never wanted the shame and guilt to hang over me or to be further victimized by having someone tell me that it was my fault or I wanted it to happen. When you tell someone that you have been sexually abused, the way they look at you changes, and that's probably what I wanted to avoid more, mostly at the beginning of a relationship. Once the relationship was settled, then it became much easier for me to tell my boyfriend, which gave him the opportunity to know me better.

Chapter 10

Promiscuity and Prisons

Childhood sexual abuse survivors are more likely to engage in risky sexual practices and are at a higher risk of HIV-infection and other sexually transmitted diseases.

The one question that I have found very difficult and rather intriguing to get an answer to is why victims of sexual abuse use sex as a means of getting over some of their emotional problems. I can truthfully admit that too often I would confuse sex for love. Just like my alcohol addiction, I have used sex as a coping mechanism to some of my most deep-seated problems. Too often, I would feel that if any of my partners decided to not have sex with me it was that they never loved me enough. I was unable to sexually commit to one partner, and there was a rush, a natural high and an undefined power whenever I engaged in random casual sex.

For most of my early twenties, I was promiscuous, and after the sexual act I would always have a feeling of emptiness and a yearning for more. But I was never too sure what "more" meant—was it more sex to fill a space in me? more connecting with someone so as to feel I belonged and I wasn't alone? Without shame or guilt, often I engaged in risky sexual practices out of abandon and seeming not to care, which led to, at twenty-three-years old, contracting a sexually transmitted disease (STD) for the first time. As it turned out, it was one of the several partners that I slept with who became infected, had gone for testing and treatment, and had given my name anonymously. I would never forget the call I received from the New York City Department of Health and Mental Hygiene and the voice of the woman on the other end who informed me in a matter-of-fact voice, but which seemed all too familiar, that I had tested positive for an STD. She advised me to see my doctor for treatment, that I was to refrain from any sexual activity until my treatment was completed, and I should inform the people I had sex with so that they too could be tested and receive treatment. The scary part of that encounter was I didn't even know I had contracted an STD, and I didn't remember who I was with to tell them to get tested.

My first visit to the health center wasn't pleasant. I was filled with denial and guilt—guilt of not knowing who I was having sex with and what other diseases they might have contracted and passed on to me. I felt foolish. I was educated, and yet I was making some rather dumb decisions that could have destroyed my life. My visits to the health center continued for about three years. One partner, who had contracted an STD and received treatment, later convinced me that I had given it to him. I had friends around me who were doing the same thing, and one after the other I would hear on the grapevine that some of my closest friends were infected with HIV. The fear of contracting HIV caused me to stop my promiscuous behavior. I didn't want to become a statistic, and I didn't want to be scared by the stigma attached to HIV.

Research has shown that there is a direct correlation between male sexual abuse and promiscuous behavior and the spread of STDs and HIV. Depression has played a major role in leading male survivors to become promiscuous, as they are more vulnerable and less likely to think about the long-term repercussion of their actions.

In the process of conducting research for this book, I identified a study that discussed childhood sexual abuse in Black men who have sex with men and the spread of HIV within the Black community.

In the study "Childhood Sexual Abuse in Black Men Who have Sex with Men: Results from Three Qualitative Studies, Cultural Diversity and Ethnic Minority" published in 2008, Dr. David Malebranche, S. D. Fields, and S. Feist-Price, revealed that there is a direct correlation between child sexual abuse and risk among men who have sex with men (MSM). Even though that actual number may vary, it is estimated that about 20 to

39 percent of child sexual abuse are among MSM. The study points out that child sexual abuse among MSM are more intense, longer and violent. Child sexual abuse has been linked to HIV risk behaviors, not only in MSM but in the general population of men who are affected by child sexual abuse, which has seen a much higher rate of unprotected receptive anal sex among MSM and men who also identify as gay or bisexual.

Recently, the media has been paying attention to the sexual abuse scandals involving Roman Catholic Church priests, but either through ignorance, complicity, or an unbreakable wall of silence, abuse in the Black and Hispanic religious communities has not been opened up. There is speculation of a racial component to the reporting, where it is suggested that since the media is generally white owned and operated and most of the victims of abuse at the hands of the priests are white, it became reportable news, and reporting of abuse in the Black or Hispanic church was not as important or relevant. From a political perspective, it is suggested in some quarters that the activist gay lobby is focusing attention on the Catholic Church's hypocrisy, seen as the source of the demonizing of homosexuality, while the abuse by its priests is covered up. My reason for making mention of the nonwhite community is not that male sexual abuse impacts this demographic any differently, rather the Church plays a fundamental role in how sexual abuse is discussed and addressed.

The recent scandal of Atlanta pastor Eddie Long, who was accused of sexually abusing men from his church, has put the Black church in the spotlight. Long is a top Black American pastor, ruling over a mega-church with a membership of over twenty-five thousand members, and an international following. As pastor, he has helped to shape the views of the Black community in regard to sexuality and how the Black community discusses male sexual abuse. He led his members in a protest march against the Georgia legislature's consideration of same-sex marriage. While the American legal system holds that Long is innocent until proven guilty, the Black church is now forced to question how it deals with sexual abuse and sexuality within the Black community.

Another self-styled leader, the so-called bishop T. D. Jakes over the years had come out against anything that hints at homosexuality and same-sex relationships, including being a part of former president George Bush's panel on faith-based communities and initiatives and publishing several books that demonize homosexuality. But, since in February 2009, his son was arrested in a park for engaging in a sex act, Jakes's silence regarding Long is noticeable.

As a Black man, who is part of the African Diaspora, I can identify with the nonwhite men in the community and fully understand why it is difficult to engage others, like me, on the issue of male sexual abuse. Notwithstanding, it should be understood that male sexual abuse is not restricted to the Black community; it is prevalent among many white and Latino communities, and just as in the Black community, it is not discussed. The victims, regardless of race or ethnicity, still suffer in silence. More and more men of color are identifying themselves as MSM, and in so doing are helping to remove the stigma of being identified as homosexuals.

Few studies have scrutinized the issues of child sexual abuse among Black MSM exclusively. Child sexual abuse is not exclusive to Black MSM. Other ethnic groups where men identify as MSM are also impacted by the poor decisions being made by victims of child sexual abuse. Many men who were victims of sexual abuse question the link between their same-sex sexual desires, behavior, and the occurrence of their abuse as children. Many often wonder if they had not been abused, whether they would still have been attracted to another of the same sex. Allowing for the limits of my research, I have come across no study to date that has demonstrated a direct correlation between male sexual abuse, child sexual abuse, and identifying as a homosexual. In fact, research has shown that there is a large percentage of homosexual men who have, at some point in their lives, experienced some level of sexual violence.

*   *   *

Another area not adequately addressed is sexual abuse in institutional settings. Prison rape, as violent sexual abuse occurring in a confined, state-run facility, is not a contemporary phenomenon; it is just as taboo as discussing male sexual abuse. With state and national incarceration policies against any sexual conduct in prisons, prohibition of protection against sexually transmitted diseases and the sexual violence that occurs as forms of preserving masculinity and relieving sexual tension, leads to the proliferation and spread of diseases including HIV. It is seen that providing condoms is akin to encouraging homosexuality.

The phenomenon prison rape—of male sexual assault—transcends ethnic and cultural boundaries. Prison rape has more to do with power and control rather than an indirect means of punishing society's "rejects." According to a 2001 Human Rights Watch study, 22 percent of male inmates have been raped at least once during their incarceration, which is an estimated 420,000 prisoners each year. These numbers reflect only those men who have actually reported the sexual assault; it is suggested by most researchers that these numbers would actually double if all victims were to actually report the crime.

Male prison-rape victims are more susceptible than any other victims of sexual abuse to contracting HIV and other sexually transmitted diseases. A 2006 report by the United Nations on drugs and crime, HIV prevention, care, treatment, and support in prison setting noted, "Reducing the transmission of HIV in prison is an integral part of reducing the spread of infection in the broader society, as any diseases contracted in prison, or medical conditions made worse by poor conditions of confinement, becomes issues of public health for the wider society when people are released."

A study conducted in 2004 by Susan Okie on US prisons and published three years later, noted that HIV prevalence in the prison system was more than four times higher than in the wider society. The US Center for Disease Control and Prevention (CDC) published in 2007 a study on sexually transmitted diseases which said that the rates of infection for Chlamydia, Gonorrhea, and Syphilis were significantly higher in prisons than in the general population.

In 2007, the United Nations Office on Drugs and Crime in a joint United Nations Program on HIV/AIDS with the World Bank presented a finding on the scope of HIV and its relation to sexual abuse in the global-wide prison systems. The document stated that of all regions in the world, sub-Saharan Africa is the hardest hit by the epidemic with almost two-thirds of all people infected with HIV living in the region. The document stressed that "HIV in prisons is both a public health and a human rights issue that needs to be addressed urgently for an effective response on the Continent. Despite this, and although there have been significant increases in national and international funding to control the epidemic, prison settings in sub-Saharan Africa have received surprisingly little attention."

The finding was intended to provide prison communities with information and a way to better reach a specific underserved population in the mainstreaming of the AIDS response throughout sub-Saharan Africa. It is suggested that the study should be used as a "common platform on which the countries themselves, as well as multilateral, bilateral and nongovernmental partners, can build coordinated policies and programs, and provide services."

The document, a work in progress, would be built upon by future contributions of other institutions and organizations for the wider dissemination of the information relation to reducing HIV in the prison system. The document is envisioned as a common platform on which the countries themselves, as well as multilateral, bilateral, and nongovernmental partners, can build coordinated policies and programs, and services. Several recommendations suggest that the document should be widely distributed to all nations and to have collaborations with institutions and organizations which would continue research to ensure implementation.

Chapter 11

Prison Rape

Prison rape not only threatens the lives of those who fall prey to their aggressors, but it is potentially devastating to the human spirit. Shame, depression, and a shattering loss of self-esteem accompany the perpetual terror the victim thereafter must endure"

—US Supreme Court Justice Harry A. Blackmun,
Farmer v. Brennan

In March 2010, I was one of the presenters at the Male Survivors 2010 International Conference which attempted to address, from a global perspective, an understanding of male sexual abuse. I spoke on advocating and working with sexually abused men of color by looking at cultural fit, outreach, and retention. I was curious to gather more information on male sexual abuse. It was my overall experience while participating on an internal panel to refocus my attention and my approach on how I would write this book. During the conference, I attended a presentation that dealt with prison rape, which opened my eyes to a group of men largely neglected within our society.

Justice Detention International is an international organization dedicated to gathering data and helping victims of prison rape. Sexual abuse outside of institutional settings rarely garners public interest, but sexual abuse behind bars has become a cause célèbre, a human-rights crisis in need of immediate attention. Cindy Struckman-Johnson and David Struckman-Johnson in 2000 acknowledged that there is little or no research on prison rape, and that an estimated 21 percent of inmates in men's prison are sexually abused at some point during their incarceration.

The 2007 survey conducted on prisons across the Unites States by Allen J. Beck and Paige M. Harrison of the Bureau of Justice Statistics (BJS) found that 4.5 percent—60,500—of the more than 1.3 million inmates held in federal prisons and state prisons had been sexually abused during the previous year. The harsh reality of the data presented by the BJS represents only a fraction of the true number of prison inmates who are victimized. It is difficult to obtain accurate data and whatever limited data exists, exposes a systemic problem and a failure within the justice system to protect the basic rights of inmates. The study reveals that victims, who are marked as fair game for attacks by other inmates, can be abused relentlessly, sometimes for long periods of time.

I have had the opportunity to speak with males who have encountered male sexual abuse in the prison system and I was informed that prisoners targeted for abuse are treated as property to be bought and sold within the prison facility by their abusers. Supporting this type of trade, most inmates are faced with the absence of preventive measures, strict enforcement of rules and regulations, which leave many defenseless and reports of rape frequently ignored. In most accounts, reports of rape are met by laughter and derision from prison officials, who often provide abusers with immunity.

Society needs to understand that anyone incarcerated for rehabilitation for crimes committed against society is likely to become a victim of sexual violence. With the exception of those who are incarcerated for extraordinary crimes and have lengthy or life sentences, most prisoners are released back into society and are prone to post-traumatic stress disorder. Studies of prison populations revealed that those who were released are likely to commit violent crimes. Many of those who have contracted some type of sexually transmitted disease while incarcerated, on release and return to their communities, are likely to infect those who they come into contact with sexually. Research has identified a direct correlation with the spread of STDs and the alarming rate of HIV, especially within minority communities as minority men account for a large percentage of men locked up behind bars.

A study of the National Commission on Correctional Health estimated that in 2002:

- 35,000-47,000 inmates were infected with HIV
- 46,000-76,000 inmates had syphilis
- 43,000 had Chlamydia
- 18,000 had gonorrhea
- 36,000 had hepatitis B
- 303,000-332,000 had hepatitis C

(All these diseases can be communicated through sexual contact)

The bulletin "HIV in prisons" by Laura M. Maruschak of the Bureau of Justice Statistics, issued on December 31, 2001, revealed that 2 percent of states prison inmates, 22,627, and 1.2 percent of federal prison inmates, 1,520, were known to be infected with HIV.

A group of researchers in their article "HIV in the United States at the turn of the century: An epidemic in transition" published in the *American Journal of Public Health*, quoted US Centers for Diseases Control and Prevention estimates of recent HIV infections at approximately 40,000 infections per year; currently there are 800,000 to 900,000 persons living with HIV. This estimation was based on the US Census Bureau 2000 Census figures of the US population of 281,422,000 and a HIV infection rate of 0.3 percent, but the HIV infection rate in US Prisons is estimated to be between 1.2 percent and 2 percent, representing four to six times higher than in the general population. The article "Characteristics of Prison Sexual Assault Targets in Male Oklahoma Correctional Facilities," published by C. Hensley and others in 2003 in the *Journal of Interpersonal Violence*, suggested that surveys of inmates have also revealed that an estimated 14 percent reported being sexually targeted by other inmates.

Stephen Donaldson in a 1995 newspaper article, "Can We Put an End to Inmate Rape," suggested that, using a rape-repeat rate conservatively estimated every other day and counting gang rapes as a single incident means at least 7,150 sexual victimizations a day in jails.

The researchers, Struckman-Johnson, suggested in a study published in an article "Sexual Coercion Rates in Seven Midwestern Prison Facilities for Men" in the December 2000 issue of *The Prison Journal*, that a substantial portion of male sexual coercion incidents, estimated to be 20 percent in larger prisons, involved prison-staff perpetrators. The study also showed that 21 percent of inmates had experienced at least one episode of pressured or forced sexual contact since being incarcerated.

A pair of researchers, Robert and Doris Dumond, in their 2002 published article "The Treatment of Sexual Assault Victims: Prison Sex" in *Practice and Policy 82*, quoted a 1994 poll reported in *The Boston Globe*, that 50 percent of survey respondents agreed that "society accepts inmate sexual assault as part of the price criminals pay for committing crimes."

A team of researchers, Martin Forst, Jeffery Fagan and T. Scott Vivona in their 1989 article "Youths in Prison and Training Schools: Perceptions and Consequences of the Treatment—Custody Dichotomy" published in the *Juvenile and Family Court Journal*, suggested that juveniles incarcerated in adult prisons are eight times more likely to commit suicide, five times more likely to be sexually assaulted, two times more likely to be assaulted by staff, and 50 percent more likely to be attacked with a weapon, as compared to juveniles in juvenile facilities.

Sexual violence in all types of detention facilities is likely to remain a growing problem as long as the public remains uninformed of the ripple effects of prison rape and fails to changes its attitude about this form of abuse.

Prison rape is not only a physically and psychologically damaging experience, it is also a formidable challenge for correctional departments attempting to secure basic human rights within correctional institutions. A study of four Midwestern states in 2000 found that about 1 in 5 inmates experiences some form of pressured or coerced sexual conduct while incarcerated (Struckman-Johnson and Struckman-Johnson, 2000). According to Stephen Donaldson, the president of the organization *Stop Prisoner Rape* (now called *Just Detention International*) and previous inmate victim of prison rape, roughly 300,000 inmates are sexually abused each year (Donaldson 1995). Courts not only recognize that "homosexual rape is commonplace" in prison, but they also make a point to depart from sentencing guidelines if they believe that a convicted felon is particular vulnerable to rape, and fits the "prisoner rape victim profile" (Man and Cronan 2001).

Prison rape is not a new phenomenon, the Home Box Office popular series *Oz* showcased life behind bars and the fight against prisoner rape. *Oz* was very popular simply because it allowed society to get a glimpse into the life of prisoners and actually gave a human approach to the struggles that inmates face behind bars. The television series, which followed the lives of the inmates in the Oswald State Correctional Facility who had been sent to the Emerald City section of the facility, held nothing back and the mature content could sometimes be overwhelming. However, the betrayal, hardships, redemption, and everything else that goes into the show makes it hard to look away.

In addition, there is a degree of skepticism towards prisoner allegations. By nature of their secretive operation, evidence is often lacking in prison rape cases, and prisoners have little bargaining power and jury support in court. This is of particular concern to those filing lawsuits, who must first pass the "deliberate indifference" test proving that correctional officials "know of and disregard an excessive risk to inmate health or safety" (Man and Cronan 2001). Inmate Roderick Keith Johnson, raped on a regular basis for one and a half years beginning on the first day that he stepped into the Allred prison unit in 2000, went to a federal court to convict prison officials for failing to protect him from cruel and unusual punishment. The quality of his evidence was called into question, despite the fact that many transfers and protection-operations for prisoners frequently lack proof of victimization.

On a more positive note, concern for prison rape seems to be increasing. The first Prison Rape laws were adopted by 18 states in 1990 in the United States of America, and by 2006, all states but Vermont now have such laws prohibiting prison rape. In 1999, the Los-Angeles-based organization Stop Prisoner Rape, now Just Detention, the American University Washington College of Law and the National Institute of Corrections implemented a joint program to more effectively prevent rape within prison. In 2003, President Bush signed the Prison Rape

Elimination Act, which created a commission to increase detection, prevention, and reduction of prisoner rape. Specifically, it:

- developed national standards to prevent, detect and reduce sexual violence in prisons
- increased correctional staff's access to data on sexual violence made prison officials more accountable for inmate safety

Furthermore, in 2005, sexual-abuse among staff in federal prisons was given stiffer penalties. It appears that the future may hold more hope for prevention of prison rape, but, as noted above, it still requires the participation and enthusiasm of the community in order to take effect. In addition, awareness is only half the battle. Implementation of practical and attitudinal support at the institutional level is another challenge altogether, and may require incentive levels for correctional officials who successfully keep rape allegations low, or penalties to those who knowingly allow allegations to remain high. The laws within some developed nations notably the United States have beeng put in place to alleviate some of these issues.

The Prison Rape Elimination Act (PREA) was passed unanimously by the United States Congress and signed into law by President Bush in 2003. This is the first federal civil law to address sexual violence behind bars, and its requirements apply to all detention facilities, both local and federal, such as state prisons, jails, lock-ups, private prison facilities, and centers for detaining illegal immigrants.

PREA states that sexual assault in detention can constitute a violation of the Eighth Amendment of the US Constitution and requires that facilities adopt a zero-tolerance approach to this form of abuse. The law calls for the development of national standards addressing prisoner rape, the gathering of nationwide statistics about the problem, the provision of grants to states to combat it, and the creation of a review panel to hold public hearings with the best and the worst performing facilities.

The organization, Just Detention International, formerly called Stop Prison Rape, gave permission for the following stories to be used to illustrate the nature of sexual abuse in prisons. Caution is advised as some of these stories are graphic, uncensored accounts of actual rapes and surrounding circumstances. The language used is raw, employs street slang, and is often upsetting. However, these accounts convey the realities of prisoner rape in ways that no statistics or abstract analyses could achieve. Additionally, these stories from victims have been given in their authentic voices, including grammatical or spelling errors.

The personal stories are written in the emotional language of the victims:

"J." from Oklahoma writes:

> I'm 16 years old. I was placed in a maximum security prison and raped several times. This keeps happening because the staff . . . will not transfer me to the right security level. The person that is raping me told me if I told anyone that he would kill me . . . The other night I tried to kill myself . . . My mind is starting to go in a world of it's own so the pain won't hurt so bad. I don't feel like a human being anymore. I'm a sexually abused animal. I should not feel this way, because I'm not supposed to be in the adult prison system. Please help me.

> I escaped [from a minimum-security institution] because older inmates were sexually harassing me. I was caught off of escape within 24 hours. The staff wrote me up an placed me in a maximum from an minimum. When I were placed in a cell . . . the convicts start yelling they were going the hit me in my butt. About a week went by then they placed an older convict . . . who waited until I were sleep laying on my stomach before he jumped on me an penetrated my butt with his penis . . . When I went to the law library they were sexually harassing me because . . . told them what happen.

> [from a complaint form for a civil rights lawsuit:] [The unit sergeant] told plaintiff do you know what happens to little boys that want to play man. In a man's prison, little boy's get their asses busted, and your a fresh 16 and I know your going to get it good. Cause I'm going to help. I know who to put in the cell with you.

"Timothy" from Virginia writes:

> Timothy C. Tucker was released from federal prison in 2001 after being traumatized by a sexual assault he says was deliberately set in motion and planned by the warden of a federal prison. The assault, he says, was "yet another example of the collusion between guards and rapists behind bars." Tucker says he was set up in retaliation for voicing concerns over the medical department and the administrative remedy procedure at the federal prison in Petersburg, Virginia.

> While housed at the Petersburg Prison, Tucker wrote letters to politicians and human rights organizations voicing his concerns over prison conditions. Because he spoke out about these issues, Tucker believes, his complaints about being sexually harassed by a fellow inmate were ignored. Moreover, after he had written several complaints he was thrown in the "hole" for 30 days under the ruse of being placed under investigation. When the 30 days were over, he was taken to the room of the man who was the subject of his complaints, a known sexual predator who was serving a 20-year sentence in a Florida prison for sexual battery of a child. He was then forced into the room under direct order of the warden, where he was raped that night.

After the sexual assault, Tucker was taken back to the "hole," where he remained for 11 days before being seen by a doctor. According to medical reports from his file, Tucker was still bleeding rectally and was suffering from significant trauma by the time he was seen. Records also indicate that the prison doctor had called several times asking to treat Tucker, but that these requests were denied; that the director of psychology and other staff members had advised the warden to separate Tucker from his sexual aggressor; and that that staff members carried out the orders of the warden under protest, stating that they were under direct orders even though they knew them to be not only wrong but criminal.

"The actions of this warden," Tucker says, "cannot go unpunished. By condoning the actions of the warden, the Justice Department sends an open invitation to prison staff and guards to use prison rape as a punishment and tool to control inmates. In this day of human rights, this behavior by our own Justice Department employees is just not acceptable."

"A. P." of Kansas says:

> At the age of 22 I was locked up . . . I was as green and wet behind the ears as they come when I went from the county jail to state prison. While in orientation an old timer took me under his wings to show me the ropes. Several weeks later he made his true intentions known . . . He told me . . . I would have to suck his dick. Upon telling him I don't do that he proceeded to give me the riot act . . .
>
> At that point a thousand and one things went through my mind. It was as though my life flashed before me. His threats and intimidation succeeded in frightening me to the degree I only wanted to survive with the least amount of pain as possible. I knew he couldn't rape me by himself. I was more afraid of how many others he would call for reinforcement. How many of them would rape me was the scariest thing of all.

"W. E." from Utah writes:

> You don't know how hard it is for me to admit this, but I was raped in the . . . county jail, by four men, It happened in [19]84, I was only 17, the act its self was a very sick, twisted, and brutal thing . . . Since then I haven't sought for any counseling, or other forms of help, and that was a very wrong decision for me, because all I've done is channel the pain, and hurt in to rage, and ended up only hurting my self even more, with more time to do. I should say, a fair estimate would be at least half, of the victims end up dead, either by the hands of a predator, for fear of prosecution, or self inflicted, for countless reasons, I almost became a statistic for the latter of the two, several times over. The years have passed, and it's still quite hard for me to confront this in any way, but I must if I'm ever to move on with my life.

"Jeremy" from Texas says:

> I was sexually assaulted by a inmate I trusted being young and not paying attention to my actions, this offender tried to buy me things also befriended me and helped me when I got sick. I woke up with this offender in my living space trying to have sexual intercourse with me, he then tried to buy me from other inmates made me go where ever he went, I wasn't supposed to go to chow without him, he was and still is a gang member. When I couldn't take it any more I told and they did a investigation and he made a statement on record that if they let him out of lock up he would do it again. I was taken to a mental facility upon release I was placed back into population on the same farm where I'd been raped after being beaten and placed in a house with a gang member of the same as my assaulter. I filed and was locked up and sent to my current farm.

"Keith" from North Carolina says:

> I was sentenced by the court . . . to be sent to a camp in Yankton, SD. The US Marshalls sent me directly to Waseca, MN FCI. It was a tough prison, I was forced to perform oral sex on some gang members due to the threat of death. I told the staff at Waseca and was sent to protective custody. They did take the investigation seriously.

> After 3 months I was sent to Butner Low Security Institution. I made friends with a man, who I fell into the trap of friendship with, then when I decided not to be friends he molested me in the wake B unit small TV room. And in my own cell 2 months later. I wonder at the trust I gave him and how people can be so. This memory will torment my soul forever. I'm in for a computer crime and the BOP put me in with molesters and hardcore rapist. My own celly [name omitted] even molested me after I got some aspirin from him. But that's what happens when you're ignorant and trust people. I write in purpose of getting this "off my chest" due to low quality psych services and the act they give me here of not believing me. A female staff member at also the FMC,

also borderline molested me, which is mind numbing. After this happened, I was sent to the Federal level Administrative Maximum Security Hospital, FMC Butner. Where I was molested by staff food service worker [name omitted]. This is an actual Bureau of Prisons staff member! A inmate molested me at the FMC (Federal Medical Center) additionally. The Butner prisons are corrupt . . . [P]eople shouldn't be deceived by the "country club" mentality about Federal Prisons going on because it's not like that at all, especially if you're stupid. I'm being sexually harassed at this moment!

"Michael Robtoy" from McNeil Island, Washington writes:

I myself am a victim of Institutional Rape. When I was 14 years old, I was committed to the California Youth Authority, where I had been repeatedly Raped by three other inmates.

Out of FEAR, SHAME, and DISGUST, I could not tell anybody what had happened to me. In my mind I had saw the attack on me as a Gay-Attack . . . . I had told myself that I could not be a Man, a Husband or even a Father . . . I was a Failure because of what I had let happen to me by the [gays] . . . I became very anti-social.

[The writer describes his first queer-bashing.] I left him laying in a pool of blood. I knew what I had done was wrong, but yet at the same time I felt good about myself. I could not understand the mixed feelings that I had. I only knew that it made me feel worth while in hurting him. From that point on, I had sought out gays in order to assault and rob them.

[The writer describes his relentless but shallow pursuit of women, his marriage, his enlisting in the Marine Corps, all in an attempt to become "A REAL MAN." He became an alcoholic. One night he was too drunk to get erect and the woman he was with, Ruth Pitts, asked:] What have you turned GAY . . . the next thing that I remember [she was a corpse.]

I meet this Homosexual [David King] who invites me to his house, and after having sex with him, he says now it is his turn, I crab him by the neck and start chocking him . . . I confess to both murders.

Upon getting off of Death Row, I was placed in the Mental Health Ward of the Penitentiary's Hospital. After many months of Counseling, and very concerned Mental Health Personal, they notice a pattern in my Criminal History, and one of the Counselors addresses the issue of Juvenile Rape, and PTSD. I was able to admit as to what had happened to me. And at that point it was like a great weight was lifted off of me.

I feel remorse over what I have done in my life, and all of the pain and suffering that I have caused others, and more so for seeking out the Gay Community and hurting them. They were not the ones who had hurt me, and for that I am sorry for what I have done to them.

If there is any way that I can bring to attention the Abuse that goes on to this day in the Juvenile Institutions throughout the United States, and train the staff to look for signs, maybe then a Child will not see what I have seen . . . If I can help one Child from seeing what I have, then my Life will not be a total waist.

The Abuse and Rapes continue to happen, and if nothing is done how many more MICHAEL ROBTOY'S will end up on Death Row. We have to address the issue of what is happening in the Juvenile Penal Institutions.

"Calvin" from California says:

I am a California State prisoner and have been incarcerated since July 7, 1964, and I too am a victim of prisoner rape . . . I am writing to you at this time to share with you my own stories of prisoner rape in hopes that this information might be beneficial in helping SPR prevent the abuse of convicted felons. Thank you for your efforts and considerations in this extremely important matter.

On or about the middle of 1965 or first part of 1966, while I was incarcerated at Soledad State Prison (Central), there was an incident at the north facility of Soledad, which involved a young white inmate, age was approximately 20 to 25, there were three black inmates who had intentions of raping this white inmate which I knew only as Snowball. To my knowledge was a straight person, and was only defending himself, killed 2 black inmates in the attack and the third one wasn't expected to live. This white inmate was referred to the district attorney who excepted the case and tried him for murder of the black inmates and was sentenced to another life term.

Approximately 1966, I was transferred to San Quentin State Prison, they (officials) let me out to general population where I was fortunate to last 20 days before I was placed in segregation where I spent better than 2 years. But during the time I was in general population while down in the education area I was approached by 3 Mexicans and forced by knife point to go with them, I was taken to an isolated area and raped by all three Mexicans afterwards was told if I told the man they would kill me.

In late 1983 or 1986, while I was returning from activities in the yard to my cell, upon opening my cell door, a black inmate forced his was into my cell and made me give him oral copulation, when it was over with the black inmate told me if I told the man he would return and hurt me.

While this was taking place the officer was sitting at the desk reading something, this I had observed when I entered my building going to my cell. This happened at California Men's Colony—East Facility San Luis California.

"David," an inmate from Massachusetts recounted his experience of being sexually abused by a female guard, which as he described, goes counter to the generally accepted belief that all sexual abuse of and by inmates is perpetuated by each other.

I think when most people think of a prisoner being raped they imagine it as male on male or male guards raping, sexually assaulting and sexually exploiting female prisoners but I do not think they realize that male prisoners are also frequently raped or sexually assaulted and exploited by female guards and prison staff and the reason it is probably not reported much, as in the case with me, is because the male prisoner is a willing participant and afraid or embarrassed to report that a woman raped him. If a male forces himself on a woman it is considered Rape however if a female forces herself upon a man it is more difficult to view it as Rape even though it actually is. I mean what male prisoner is going to complain about being Raped, sexually assaulted exploited and having sex with a woman while in prison? It's like if a female Guard wants to punch a male prisoner in the mouth 5 times, rip-off his pants and get down and perform oral sex on him or force and order him to perform oral sex or intercourse on her, how many male prisoners would complain and not willingly participate, as I did even though they were in fact Raped, sexually assaulted, assaulted, abused or exploited. Male prisons are full of men who are horny and think about and miss women and female companionship like 24 hours a day and they are also full of female Guards and staff who are well aware of, sense and are attracted to the wanting desire that these horny men show towards them which is much more attention and wanting desire that men who are regularly with women on the outside show them and the female staff are also privy to constantly seeing the male prisoners naked, showering, masturbating, etc . . . and are able to view their wares in all shapes, sizes and colors like a kid in a candy store and if they see something they like they often exploit it and their power over the prisoner and help themselves which may include Rape, sexual assault, assault, exploitation, abuse, etc . . . However willing the male prisoner may be. When I have been Raped, sexually assaulted, assaulted, exploited, abused, etc . . . by a female prison Guard numerous times I was shocked yet willing for craving and want of sex with a woman yet the more it occurred the more abused, used, exploited, etc . . . I felt.

Bill Clements Unit
9601 SPUR 591Amarillo, TX 79107

An inmate, who chose to remain anonymous, shared the following in a letter:

Dear Reader,

I would like to tell you all a little story. A long time ago as a young man of about eighteen or nineteen years old. I had a very unfortunate and horrifying experience where I was arrested and charged with a crime of which I had no knowledge of at all. I was only about 5'9"-125 lbs skinny as a rail and what you'd call very nice looking somewhat with delicate features. Anyway my first introduction to prison life was how good you could fight or if some booty bandit wanted to try to make you his girlfriend. And not even thinking or knowing anything about prison life at all I was given a bunk in this cell with seven other guys all older and ex-cons. As soon as the count was made and the guards had there walk by, all of the guys raped me repeatedly all night and everyday for about two weeks until the county jail released me on bond. Charges against me were eventually dismissed for nothing relating me to the crime of robbery. It was later found out to be someone's idea of a joke. I never told anyone this and have tried to suppress it all my life or forget it ever happened. Sometimes I get depressed and have to take psychiatric medication to have me forget because I can go off the deep end and get filled with helpless rage or anger. I've even contemplated suicide several times, hopefully there are others out there who would like to sit down and let me explain how I feel and other things I've kept bottled up inside for all these years just begging to be released. Please write to me cause I need someone to write too and talk with at times about things that I've never even told my family about and I promise to write back.

Another inmate, "R. J. Johnson," writes:

By knowing that I would never be able to step outside the confines of prison again in my life, (there is no natural life sentence in the state of Texas, but I have a de facto natural life sentence) I have the mind-set that prison is my Home and I have to adjust and just overlook a lot of things that I see and things that are done to inmates, not only by other inmates but by other officers done to, for and against inmates, that are illegal, immoral, and against the very rules that they purport and claim to be enforcing. But while you have a de facto natural life sentence you ask yourself, how many times can you do that? how many times can you turn a blind eye to injustice? how many times can you ignore the irony and hypocrisy? how many times can you accept being subjected to injustice and not speak out even though the courts, both civil and criminal as well as good portion of society gives its tacit approval to the mistreatment of prisoners. Look at the Gitmo and Abu Ghraib prisoner scandals; does any one notice that some of those soldiers were state prison officers?

Well all of these thoughts caused me to want to speak out. I started by writing what are called grievances, after figuring out that the grievances were only a state system to identify and harass the person who wrote it, and find a way to deny the claims brought forth there in. So I filed a law suit on the harassment and retaliation that I was receiving there from my efforts.

Yet on March 24, 2005 after I had filed a law suit. A law suit on several prison officers that had stole my wedding band and used sophistry to circumvent the rules acts of malfeasance and misfeasance, to cover up their criminal acts against me, I was told by one of the officers that the federal judges over this region were in with the officers on this unit, so it is a waste of time to even pursue that route just accept what was done to you and move on! I couldn't continue to accept things and move on so I filed the law suit, and after I was called to a hearing on it, almost a month later, on the date of March 24, 2005, I was taken out of my cell, beat with night sticks, taunted, and one of the officers crammed a night stick in my anus, while yelling, all "nigger" like it in the ass, you like that, nigger boy? I was not given any medical treatment and I was sent back to my cell the officers were laughing and stating I should file a law suit on that. I gathered the names of several witnesses that would testify, hoping that I would at least get transferred while an investigation was launched, so that I could begin some sort of healing process. My mail was being stopped, (and probably still is), I was able to sneak word out to the court handling the law suit against the same officers that sexually assaulted me. and inform the judge that my mail was being blocked to the court, and that I wanted to file the protection order, that was enclosed in the transmission that I had snuck out to the court and why I had to sneak it out. I explained to the court that I had been sexually assaulted by some of the same officers that were named in the original complaint and that I needed the court to act in order to continue to prosecute my claims and be safe from further assaults.

In disbelief the court did absolutely nothing, and informed the officers at the unit that I snuck out a letter to the court, the judge further warned me about sneaking out any other letters to the court. I haven't had any sleep for the past several weeks, I awaken after an hour or so reliving the assault, I can feel it in my sleep as if it is happening all over again. I haven't told family or friends because I have none, after receiving this sentence, wife, kids and family buried me in the grave yard of their minds as if I was dead and had died eight years ago. I doubt if I am even a passing fancy in any of their conversations . . . Well I really can't explain why and how a federal judge could ignore this and not even report a crime. It seems as if it is a crime itself, in what this judge has done.

It there is any one reading this, and can help me receive some justice from what these parasites have done to me, please write to me I would like to here from any one willing to help.

I have ran up against a brick wall and a well organized oppressive system.

You may contact me at the address below.

Robertson Unit
12071 F.M. 3522
Abilene, TX 79601

Conclusion

In order to change social perception of male sexual abuse it is important that more victims of male sexual abuse speak up. Sexual abuse has more to do with power and control and less about the sexual act.

I hope that the stories presented throughout the chapters in this book have offered some inspiration and stimulated reflection on how society regards and treats men who are sexually abused. The stories have put a human face on what would otherwise be bland, dry, academic research and statistics. But, those stories of male sexual abuse are not limited to any one ethnic, racial, cultural, religious, social, or economic group within society. Male sexual abuse, like that which is practiced on females, has more to do with power and control and less about the sexual act or sexual orientation. One very interesting point that should be taken from the stores is that most of the victims and survivors were sexually abused by family members or close family friends—the familiar or the trusted. It is important, as a takeaway, to note that there is a thin line delineating the difference between a victim and a survivor as it relates to the abuse. A victim is the result of the act when it was perpetuated; a survivor is someone who is a victim but who has been able to process and reconcile aspects of the abuse and move on with life. Nonetheless, a person who has been sexually abused is forever a victim.

It is critical to note that sexual abuse is the breakdown of trust, a double-edged sword that allows the abuser to take control, and it condemns the victim to silence. Trust, in this context, builds a sense of fear within the mind of the victims and prevents him or her from speaking up or seeking help. Since most often the perpetrator is well known or an adult trusted by the family that victims are often afraid that no one would believe them.

Finkelhor and Browne in 1985 discussed four dynamics of sexual abuse, "stigmatization, betrayal, traumatic sexualization and powerlessness." In one of the stories, of the young man who was sexually abused by his father for years, he found it difficult to tell his mother, because he was afraid she would not believe him and instead blame him for encouraging his father's attentions; the other boys who were molested by family members found it difficult to speak up because they too, never felt anyone would believe them. I came to realize that in my experience of rape, that my abuser took his time to mold me—he manipulated and enticed me to trust him.

In the previous chapters, I discussed relationship between homosexuality and male sexual abuse. Too often I am asked if my sexual abuse has had an impact on my identifying as gay or allowing me to engage in same-sex relationships. There are also those who question how I could enjoy the company of a man sexually after all that had happen to me. While there is no single or simple answer to any of those questions, I know for a fact that there was a point when I engaged in same—sex relationship out of revenge and as an attempt to relive my abuse. There was also a period in my life when I had felt that no woman would want to be with me because of what had occurred. I also felt that I was dirty, scarred for life, and I had convinced myself that the sexual abuse and rape occurred because I was suppressing my true identity, which my abusers exploited to their advantage. I know that my sexual identity has nothing to do with my abuse; I have accepted myself as gay, and that is who I am.

Toward the end of writing this book, I decided that I needed to go back to therapy. I need help. I still have unresolved issues that I have to address. I am still struggling with trust, accepting love, and feelings that I will ever live a normal life. After all the stories that I heard and the number of men I met who shared their stories with me, I needed to debrief and regroup. The one question that I am yet to answer is: why I still draw a line between my definition of love and sex? Why do I still feel ashamed of myself for the promiscuous lifestyle I once lived and the things I did to cope with my depression? My journey is not yet over, but I have stability and I have learned to forgive myself for believing that the abuse was my fault. There is no single answer to how to move on or recover; I'm still in the trial and error stage. Not all coping mechanisms are going help everyone, and at times it takes a sense of creativity.

As I mentioned earlier in the book, I am neither a clinician nor do I have all the answers of how to cope with sexual abuse or the various ways to cope with sexual abuse as a man. I can share four key points that worked for me:

- Confrontation
- Resolution
- Accountability
- Forgiveness

Confrontation is when you let the abuser know that you know that he or she did something wrong to you. Even if it is a family member or close family friend, it is important to let him or her know. Let your abuser know that not only was his or her actions illegal they were also morally wrong. Make it very clear that you did not deserve the abuse, and that it was not your fault. It is important to explain to the abuser how their actions have affected your life and how their actions made you feel as a victim of the abuse. You can also suggest to your abuser how you may want him or her to be answerable for his or her actions. A written apology may be more poignant, as it is something to hold on to, and the abuser may be better able to express his or her thoughts in writing. A verbal apology may be traumatic and a difficult process, but there are those who may get a greater sense of relief when they actually hear their abuser say that they are sorry for what they did and how their actions impacted your life.

Depending on the circumstances and your levels of support, you may need a trusted friend or family member with you. When you make your request, allow the person the chance to respond. It is very critical to understand that he or she may not respond to you, and they may deny that the abuse every occurred. The response may not be what you wanted to hear, and this may make you angry or upset. The most important thing to understand is that once you have said your part and the response isn't what you were expecting or can deal with, immediately walk away. You should never feel obliged to hang around.

I remember very clearly the day I confronted the man who raped me when I was fourteen. I had several text conversations with him, and on a weekend trip back to my home, I asked if I could meet him at his job. When I walked in, I could see lust in his eyes, and he immediately asked what my plans were for the evening. I was very uncomfortable and ashamed to be in his presence. My emotions were mixed as a part of me was still in love with him and another part of me hated what he had done to me. When I asked him why he violated me and if he felt I was gay, he replied that he knew I wanted it, and he noted that I had that look. He was unable to say what that look was but added that I was the first person he had abused, I would never forget him, and that he could get me whenever he wanted. I knew at that moment that he had some serious mental issues. I was aware then that he had and continued to molest other young boys in the neighborhood.

I felt remorse and I wished I had the strength to speak about what he had done to me and to report him, since I knew that he was molesting other boys. I decided that I would wait until I was older and try and see if I could have the conversation again. When I moved to New York, I tried reaching out to him but he was more interested in reliving the past. I would never have the opportunity of talking with him again because he was murdered in 2009. While some members of my family were elated that he was dead, I felt sadness inside me. Perhaps it is survivor's guilt, but I still miss him.

Resolution by definition means the act or process of bringing a problem to conclusion. For victims of sexual abuse, resolution may have several different definitions and meanings. There are those who feel determined to confront their abusers or reunite with their abuser and those who may be aware of the abuse. For others it could be cutting all ties with dysfunctional family members or situations and working on developing new, healthy relationships. In my experience, resolution meant forgiving myself, that the abuse was my fault, and forgiving my abusers for what they did to me. It was also a way for me to let go of my past and the memories that haunted me.

In the process of finding resolution, it is important to seek some form of professional help. Therapy can be a very cathartic process, which, through reliving the experiences, allows victims an opportunity to discuss in a nonjudgmental way how they feel about the abuse and how it has affected their lives. Therapy helps victims develop coping strategies to become survivors and allows those who were abused to confront their fears. It is crucial to note that it is okay to walk away from family members who blame you for the abuse or those who believe that it was your fault. If you are a part of one of those dysfunctional families where you are asked to remain silent out of a need to protect the family from shame or guilt, it is perfectly okay to cut ties with those family members. This is about your own survival as a person. Victims of sexual abuse should never allow themselves to be convinced by anyone that they are in the wrong and neither should they allow themselves to be second guessed.

Accountability is no easy task. It is one of the most difficult challenges for victims. It is never easy holding a family member or a close family friend accountable for something they did to you. It becomes even more problematic when you have to see your abuser at family functions or your family refuses to acknowledge that the abuse occurred. If victims are fortunate to have their abusers acknowledge the abuse, it is imperative that they are held accountable for their actions. A simple apology "I'm sorry" is never enough. Reporting the abuser to the police and filing criminal charges against him with the possibility of a court trial may be difficult for the victim, who may be forced to relive in graphic detail what happened, but it is one way of ensuring that the abuser would not commit the same crime again.

My suggestion is that abusers should seek professional help because they need it. I am not one to argue about monetary compensation, and I do not place any monetary value on my life or on the abuse I suffered. It would be a good idea that victims ask the abuser to volunteer time and services to their immediate community. Time lost can never be regained, but the abuser can give back in some positive way to society. I would ask my abusers to donate to a charity of my choosing and in so doing give them an opportunity to help other survivors for the lives they have destroyed.

Forgiveness was the key to my recovery and survival. Victims need first to learn to forgive themselves for believing that the abuse was their fault. Second, forgive the abusers. It is pointless living your life with shame and guilt and blaming your survivor while he or she may be living a happy functional life, which would deprive you of your own inner peace and happiness. Forgiveness wasn't easy for me; it took years of guilt, denial, and sporadic periods of depression to finally realize that I was not at fault. I would walk around with a chip on my shoulder, thinking that the world owed me something because someone wronged me and took my childhood innocence. When I was twenty-four-years-old, I was given a book by Larry Kramer (a leading gay activist who helped to form Gay Men Health Crisis) which helped me realize, as he said, "Maturity comes when we have learned to accept the things in life we have little or no control over." I had an "A ha!" moment. I may not be able to change the hands of time, and I should not have to live the rest of my life filled with anger and hatred over what someone did to me.

The most difficult question to ask oneself is how I can forgive someone who destroyed my life, how can I forgive someone who won't even acknowledge the offense, or even ask for forgiveness? I am not a religious man, but I do believe in the teachings of the Bible. Isn't it our right not to want to forgive someone for the wrong done to us? If we don't forgive, we are likely to live the rest of our lives with anger, and that is not healthy. Most of the guys I interviewed or who contributed to the book found it very difficult to forgive. It's never an easy process, but it helps to set us free.

The important thing to note is that forgiveness has nothing to do with the abuser; it has more to do with the victim/survivor. Forgiveness releases the victim from the shame and guilt and all that they have been through. Once we have started the process of forgiving, we are on the right path to correcting the belief that it was our fault and releasing the hold that the abuser and the action still have on us. It will take time; this will not happen overnight. Forgiveness does not mean that we are going to forget.

I suggest that those who are religious should read their Bibles and become more involved in their church and community. Forgiveness has more to do with faith and courage. It will help to set you free; it will let you feel lighter; it will bring freedom; and it will be a form of self-empowerment. If my grandmother were alive, she would have told me that vengeance is left up to God and Him alone. Forgiving your abuser is likely to give you a greater level of understanding of the act and the person who did it to you. Change comes when we accept and acknowledge that there is a problem.

As survivors of sexual abuse, it is important that we, too, give back to our communities by putting a face and a voice to the cause of ending sexual abuse and give courage to speak out to those who may still be suffering in silence. It is through our strength and courage that we are able to save lives and put a human face to the cause. This journey that I have undertaken was never going to be easy, but I know for sure that through my story, I may have saved a life. Even if I have only the opportunity of saving one life, I am satisfied in the knowledge that I was able to make a contribution to humanity. I live by the teachings of "The Secret"; I have come to the realization that everything in life happens for a reason. It was fear that has led me to my journey, and I am learning each day how to overcome my fears.

Appendix A

Male Survivors of Sexual Violence

Published by the **Michigan Resource Center on Domestic and Sexual Violence**

The Michigan Resource Center on Domestic and Sexual Violence is a collaboration of the **Michigan Domestic Violence Prevention and Treatment Board** and the **Michigan Coalition Against Domestic and Sexual Violence**.
http://www.resourcecenter.info/files/stats/Male%20Survivors.pdf

Awareness of Male Sexual Assault
Awareness of male sexual assault is increasing and becoming more frequently studied and talked about. The general invisibility of the rape of boys and men is due in part to widespread homophobia and societal definitions of masculinity and maleness. Systems of dominance, homophobia and gender rigidity not only perpetuate sexual violence, these systems of power serve to silence male survivors who may fear appearing powerless, weak and unmasculine.

The rape of men and boys is an act of power used to reinforce the dominant status of the perpetrator through the use of sexual violence. Males perceived as powerless become targets of these assaults. Young boys, adolescent men, men in institutions and men with disabilities are particularly vulnerable to this form of violence. Contrary to the belief that homosexual men commit male-to-male sexual violence, research shows that men who identify as heterosexual are overwhelmingly the perpetrators of male sexual assault.

Statistics show that heterosexual men commit 96-98% of all sexual violence against males and females.

Prevalence of Sexual Assault Perpetrated Against Boys and Men

Increased attention and awareness of sexual violence and the growing recognition of male victimization in particular have led to an increase in the number of studies being conducted on the prevalence of sexual assault of boys and men. Research suggests that sexual violence perpetrated against boys and men is widespread with estimates ranging from one in five to one in eight males reporting some form of sexual assault. A majority of studies confirm that an estimated 5-10% of boys and men will be raped in their lifetime. Using a definition of rape that includes forced vaginal, oral or anal sex, the National Violence Against Women Survey found that 1 of 33 US men had experienced an attempted or completed rape as a child or an adult (Tjaden, Patricia and Nancy Thoennes (1998).

Perpetrators of Sexual Assault

The majority of perpetrators of sexual violence are men. Studies of sexual assault against children and young adolescents report that more than 97% of perpetrators were male. Despite popular belief, most male perpetrators identify themselves as heterosexual and often have consensual sexual relationships with women. One study notes that 98% of male perpetrators self-identify as heterosexual (Lisak, D., Hopper, J., Song, P, 1996). The vast majority (over 80%) of sexually abused boys never become adult perpetrators, while a majority of perpetrators (up to 80%) were abused as boys and young men. Perpetrators tend to be known by, but unrelated to; the victim (Holmes, W. C. & Slap, G. B., JAMA 1998) Females can also be perpetrators. Studies report that women commit 2-4% of reported sex offenses against children. A Bureau of Justice Statistics study reports that overall, 6% of offenders who sexually assaulted juveniles were female, and compared with just 1% who sexually assaulted adults (Washington, DC: Bureau of Justice Statistics, 2000). Female perpetrators of sexual assault tend to use persuasion rather than force or the threat of force during their crimes (Holmes, W. C. & Slap, G. B., JAMA 1998).

Boys and Adolescent Males

According to a report on the sexual assault of young children reported to law enforcement that used data from the National Incident-Based

Reporting System, more than half of all juvenile victims of sexual assault were under age 12 and one of every seven victims of sexual assault were under the age of 6. According to the Bureau of Justice Statistics, the year in a male's life when he is most likely to be a victim of sexual assault is the age of 4 (Washington, DC: Bureau of Justice Statistics, 2000). Twenty six percent of sexual assault victims under the age of 12 and 8% of sexual assault victims aged 12 to 17 are boys (Washington, DC: Office of Justice Programs, 1999).

Interpersonal Relationships

Sexual assault in interpersonal relationships is an extremely prevalent form of violence, particularly when we consider that men involved in physically abusive relationships with other men may be especially vulnerable to sexual assaults by their partners. In a study of 162 gay men and 111 lesbian women, 52% reported at least one incident of sexual coercion by same-sex partners. Lesbian women experience 1.2 incidents per person while gay men experience 1.6 incidents per person (Waldner-Haugrud, Lisa and Vaden Gratch, Linda, 1997). Nearly 7 million men are raped and/or physically assaulted by an intimate partner in their lifetime. Each year, 834,000 men are sexually assaulted by their partners (Tjaden, Patricia and Nancy Thoennes (1998).

Rape and sexual assault of men and boys occurs in other all-male settings including military organizations, athletics, dormitories and fraternities. All-male environments cultivate the tendency for violence perpetrated by men against women and against other men (Scarce, Michael, 1997). A sense of competition, violence as a rite of passage, an expression of dominant status or power, or an initiation or hazing are among the many reasons this culture of violence exists in these settings.

Sexual Assault in Prisons

The few studies that have been done on prison rape reveal astonishing rates of abuse. A recent study of prisons in four Midwestern states found that approximately 20% of male inmates reported a pressured or forced sex incident while incarcerated. About 9% of male inmates reported that they had been raped (Stop Prison Rape accessed 2/18/03). Stop Prison Rape estimates that 360,000 men are sexually assaulted or raped in prisons in the United States each year. For at least two of the three inmates who are sexually assaulted, the assaults are not isolated incidents but a pattern repeated on daily basis (Scarce, Michael, 1997). Sexual assaults in prisons and other correctional institutions are perpetrated by corrections officers and staff as well as by other inmates. Sexual violence perpetrated in a prison setting is often committed by men who identify as heterosexual as a tool to establish and maintain power and control over other men. Shockingly, prison rape is often not included in the Bureau of Justice Statistics crime surveys or estimates of rape and sexual assault.

Male Survivors of Sexual Violence

Boys and Men with Disabilities
Studies show that boys and men with disabilities are twice as likely as boys and men without disabilities to be sexually abused in their lifetime (Statistics Canada, Centre for Justice Statistics, 2001). More than 90% of men and women with developmental disabilities will experience sexual abuse at some point in their lives. Forty-nine percent will experience 10 or more abusive incidents (Valenti-Hein, D. & Schwartz, L, 1885). Reported rates of sexual violence range from 4-6% among adolescent boys with disabilities (Holmes, W. C. & Slap. *JAMA*, 1998). Other studies suggest that 16-30% of boys with disabilities will be sexually abused before their eighteenth birthday.

Impact on Male Survivors
Boys and men who are sexually assaulted may experience a wide range of post-traumatic symptoms including depression, Post-Traumatic Stress Disorder (PTSD), and other emotional and physical problems as a result. Common reactions of men and boys after an assault can also include fear of appearing "unmasculine," societal, peer or self-questioning of their sexuality, homophobia, sense of shame, and feelings of denial.

All-Male Cultural Institutions
Rape and sexual assault of men and boys occurs in other all-male settings including military organizations, athletics, dormitories and fraternities. All-male environments cultivate the tendency for violence perpetrated by men against women and against other men. A sense of competition, violence as a rite of passage, an expression of dominant status or power,

or an initiation or hazing are among the many reasons this culture of violence exists in these settings.

Help for Male Survivors

The sexual violence perpetrated against boys and men is severely underreported and this group of survivors is underserved. Boys and men who are sexually assaulted rarely see their reality reflected in articles, books or in direct service program outreach initiatives, which further isolates them and reinforces the devastating myths surrounding male survivors of sexual assault. Resources are becoming increasingly more available for male survivors, their friends and families, and professionals who work with them. Familiarize yourself and your organization with resources in the community so you will be prepared to help male survivors in their journey through healing.

References

References for Michigan Resource Center on Domestic and Sexual Violence

Holmes, W. C. & Slap, G. B., (1998) "Sexual Abuse of Boys: Definition, Prevalence, Sequelae, and Management." *Journal of the American Medical Association.* 1998; 280 (21): 1855-1872.

Lisak, D., Hopper, J., Song, P. (1996) "Factors in the cycle of violence: Gender Rigidity and Emotional Constriction." *Journal of Traumatic Stress.* 1996; 9: 721-743.

Scarce, Michael, (1997) *Male on Male Rape: The Hidden Toll of Stigma and Shame.* New York, New York: Insight Books, 1997.

Sobsey, D, (1994) *Violence and abuse in the lives of people with disabilities: The end of silent acceptance?* Baltimore: Paul H. Brookes Publishing Co., 1994 in People with Mental Retardation & Sexual Abuse by

Leigh Ann Reynolds, MSSW, MPA accessed on 2/18/03 at http://thearc.org/faqs/Sexabuse.html.

Tjaden, Patricia and Nancy Thoennes, (1998) *Prevalence, Incidence and Consequences of Violence Against Women.* Washington, DC: National Institute of Justice, Centers for Disease Control and Prevention.

Valenti-Hein, D. & Schwartz, L, (1995) *The sexual abuse interview for those with developmental disabilities.* James Stanfield Company. Santa Barbara: California, 1995.

Waldner-Haugrud, Lisa and Vaden Gratch, Linda, (1997) "Sexual Coercion in Gay/Lesbian Relationships: Descriptives and Gender Differences." *Violence and Victims.* 1997; 12(1): 87-98.

Statistics Canada, Centre for Justice Statistics (2001) 1994 in Transcending Silence Series by the Wisconsin Coalition Against Sexual Assault, 2001.

Stop Prison Rape accessed 2/18/03 at www.spr.org.

Washington, DC: Bureau of Justice Statistics, (2000) Sexual Assault of Young Children as Reported to Law Enforcement: Victim, Incident, and Offender Characteristics.

Washington, DC: Office of Justice Programs, (1999) *Juvenile Offenders and Victims: 1999 National Report.*

Reference

Allen, B. 1996. *Rape Warfare*. Minneapolis: University of Minnesota Press.

Allen, J. Beck and Paige M. Harrison. 2007. Bureau of Justice Statistics. "Sexual Victimization in State and Federal Prisons Reported by Inmates."

Altman, D. R. The effects of Childhood Sexual Abuse on Adult Male Attachments in close Relationships. A Dissertation. Texas A & M University. August 2005.

Amnesty International. 2001. *Abuse of Women in Custody: Sexual Misconduct and Shackling of Pregnant Women.*

Andersen. 2005. "A Particular Case of Possible: Sexual Abuse in Adolescence—A Story of Overcoming." *Qualitative Social Work* 4 (3): 253-69.

Axley, M. 1992. "Male Sexual Abuse Too Long Ignored." *The Skanner* 17 (49): 1.

Batterfield, F. 2003. "Infections in Newly Freed Inmates Are Rising Concern: What do we know about HIV in African Prisons." United Nations office on Drug Crime and Joint United Nations Program on HIV/AIDS.

Banyard, W. and Siegal, l. 2004 "Childhood Sexual Abuse: A Gender Perspective on Context and Consequences." *Child Maltreatment* 9 (3): 223-38

Black, Cheryl, and Deblassie, R. Sexual abuse in male children and adolescents: indicators, effects, and treatments." *Adolescence, Spring,* (1993).

Bureau of Justice Statistics. 2004. "Sexual Violence Reported by Correctional Authorities." http://www.ojp.usdoj.gov/bjs/abstract/ svrca04.htm

Buzi, R. and Peggy, S. 2007. "The relationship between adolescent depression and a history of sexual abuse." *Adolescence* 42: 168.

Carroll, L.J. (2009). *Sexuality Now: Embracing Diversity.* Wadsworth Publishing. 3rd Edition.

Chapleau, O. and Russell, D. 2008. "Male rape myths: The role of gender, violence and sexism." *Journal of Interpersonal Violence* 23: 600-15.

Chen, X. Johnson, K. Hoyt, D. Whitbeck, L. *Victimization and Posttraumatic Stress Disorder among Runaway and Homeless Adolescents. 22:6 (2007) pg. 721-734.* Lincoln: Sociology Department of University of Nebraska, Lincoln. 2007.

Christopher, D. Man and Cronan, John P. 2001. "Forecasting sexual abuse in prison: The prison subculture of masculinity as a backdrop for 'deliberate indifference'." *Journal of Criminal Law and Criminology* (42 U.S.C. 15601 (13), 15602(1). (42 U.S.C. 15602).

Davies, M. and John, A. 2006. "Effects of perpetrator gender and victims sexuality on blame towards male victims of sexual assault." *The Journal of Social Psychology* 146 : 275-291.

Donaldson, Stephen. "Can We Put an End to Inmate Rape." *USA Today,* May 1, 1995.

Dumond, Robert and Dumond, Doris 2002. "The Treatment of Sexual Assault Victims." *Prison Sex: Practice and Policy 82.* Lynne Reinner Publishers, Inc.

Ehrenreich, B. 1997. *Blood Rites.* New York: Holt Metropolitan.

Fields, Sheldon D.; Malebranche, David; Feist-Price, Sonja. "Childhood Sexual Abuse in Black Men Who have Sex with Men: Results from Three Qualitative Studies, Cultural Diversity and Ethnic Minority" Psychology, Volume. 14. Number. 4. October 2008. Pages 385-390.

Finkelhor, J. (1987). "The Trauma of Child Sexual Abuse: Two Models". J Interpers Violence. December (1987). Vol. 2. No. 4. Pages 348-366.

Finkelhor, Hotaling, Lewis and Smith, (1990); In Understanding the Complexity of Childhood Sexual Abuse: A Review of the Literature With Implications for Family Counseling. Hunter, S. V. The Family Journal. October 2006. Vol. 14. No. 4. Pages 349-358.

Forst, M. Fagan, J. and T, Scott Vivona. (1989). "Youths in Prison and Training Schools: Perceptions and Consequences of the Treatment-Custody Dichotomy." *Juvenile and Family Court Journal* 40: 1-14.

Foubert, J. and Cremedy, B. 2006. "Reactions of men of color to a commonly used rape prevention program: Attitude and predicted behavior changes." *Sex Roles* 57: 137-44

Frazier, P. A. and Schauben, L. 1994. In "Perception of male victims in depicted sexual assault: A review of the literature" 2006 by Michelle Davies and Paul Rogers. *Aggression and Violent Behavior* 11 (4): 367-77.

Goosby A. 2004. "The Incarcerated: A Report from the 12th World AIDS Conference; Stubblefield E, Wohl D (2000). Prisons and Jails Worldwide: Update from the 13th International Conference on AIDS.

Graham, R. 2006. "Male rape and the careful construction of the male victim." *Social and Legal Studies* 15 (2): 187-208.

Grossman, F. K. 2002. In *Male-on-Male Rape of an Adult Man: A Case Review and Implication for Interventions* by Danny G. Willis. 2009. *Journal of the American Psychiatric Nurses Association* 14(6): 454-461.

Grossman, F. 2003."Male rape victims need to speak out." *Boston Globe.* A20.

Groth, A. N. 1979. In *The Secrecy of Child Sexual Abuse* by Nancy Faulkner. 1996. *Sexual Counseling Digest 10/96.*

Groth, A. N. 1979. *In Men Who Rape: The Psychology of the Offender.* New York: Plenum.

Hagan and McCarthy, (1997). Event History Analysis of Antecedents to Running Away from Home and Being on the Street. American Behavioral Scientist. September 2001 Vol. 45. Pages 51-65.

Hall, K. 2008. "Childhood sexual abuse and adult sexual problems: A new view of assessment and treatment." *Feminism and Psychology* 18 (4): 546-56.

Harry, Joseph. 1992. "Conceptualizing Anti-Gay Violence," in Gregory Herek Gregory and Kevin Berrill, eds. *Hate Crimes: Confronting Violence Against Lesbians and Gay Men.* Newbury Park, CA: Sage Publications.

Hartil, M. 2009. "The Sexual Abuse of Boys in Organized Male Sports." *Men and Masculinity.* 2009. Vol. 12. No. 2. Pages 225-249

Hartill, M. 2008. "The sexual abuse of boys in organized male sports." *Man and Masculinities.* 2008. Vol. 10. Pages 1-25.

Hensley, C., Tewksbury, R., and Castle, T. 2003. "Characteristics of Prison Sexual Assault Targets in Male Oklahoma Correctional Facilities." *Journal of Interpersonal Violence* 18:595-606.

Hillman, Richard J., O'mara, Nigel, Taylor-Robinson, David, Harris J. R,. Medical and Social Aspects of Sexual Assault of Males: A survey of 100 Victims. *British Journal of General Practice, December*, 1990.

Hodge and Cantor, (1998); in Perception of male victims in depicted sexual assaults: A review of the literature. *Aggression and Violent Behavior*. Volume 11, Issue 4, July -August 2006. Pages 367-377.

Hoyt, D.R., Whitebeck, L.B., & Yoder, K.A. Impact of Family abuse on running away deviance, and street victimization among homeless rural and urban youth. *Childe Abuse and Neglect*. Volume 30, Issue 10, October 2006, Pages 1117-1128.

Hoyt, Ryan, and Cauce, (1999). Event History Analysis of Antecedents to Running Away from Home and Being on the Street. American Behavioral Scientist. September 2001 Vol. 45. Pages 51-65.

Hunter, Mic. 1991 *"Abused Boys: The Neglected Victims of Sexual Abuse"*Random House Publishing Group.

Human Rights Watch. 2002. World Report; Human Rights Watch (1999). World Report. Special Programs and Campaigns—Prisons.

Human Rights Watch (1999). World Report. Special Programs and Campaigns—Prisons.

_____ 2001. *"No Escape: Male Rape in USA Prisons"*. Human Rights Watch Report, April 2001.
FindLaw. http://www. hrw.org/reports/2001/prison/report.html

International Centre for Prison Studies. 2007. *The World Female Imprisonment List*. London, King's College.

_____ 2007. *The World Prison Population List*. London, King's College.

Kantor, E. 2006. *HIV Transmission and Prevention in Prisons*. University of California San Francisco. Retrieve on September 2007 http://hivinsite.ucsf.edu/InSite?page=kb-07-04-13.

Karon, John M., Fleming, Patricia L.,Steketee, Richard W.,De Cock, Kevin M. 2001. "HIV in the United States at the Turn of the Century: An Epidemic in Transition." *American Journal of Public Health* 91(7):1060-1068.

Kassing, L. and Prieto, L. 2009. "The rape myth and blame-based beliefs of counselors-in-training towards male victims of rape." *Journal of Counseling and Development,* 8 (1): 455-61.

Kelson, G. 1999. *Gender and Immigration.* New York: New York University Press.

Key, D. P. Instrumental Sexual Scripting: An Examination of Gender-Role Fluidity in the Correctional Institution. Journal of Contemporary Criminal Justice. August 2002. Vol. 18. No. 3. Pages 258-278

King and Woolett, (1997) in Perception of male victims in depicted sexual assaults: A review of the literature. *Aggression and Violent Behavior.* Volume 11, Issue 4, July-August 2006. Pages 367-377.

Lehner E (2001). Hell Behind Bars: The Crime That Dare Not Speak Its Name.

Light, D. and Monk-Turner, E. (2009). Circumstances Surrounding Male Sexual Assault and Rape: Findings From the National Violence Against Women Survey. Journal of Interpersonal Violence. November 2009. Vol. 24. No. 11. Page. 1849-1858.

Light and Kirt (2000). In Hartil, M. The Sexual Abuse of Boys in Organized Male Sports. *Men and Masculinity.* October 2009. Vol. 12. No. 2. Pages 225-249

Ling, L. H. M. 2001. *Postcolonial International Relations: Conquest and Desire Between Asia and the West.* London: Palgrave.

Losch, William C. "Prison Rape: Our Wake-up Call: Crime and Media." http://www.fsu.edu/~crimdo/losch.html (6-24-03)

Penzell, Dennis H. 1985. "Child Abuse and Neglect." *Journal of the American Medical Association (JAMA) 1985; 254: 796-800*

Macher A,. 2004. "The Incarcerated: A Report from the 12th World AIDS Conference; Stubblefield E, Wohl D (2000). Prisons and Jails Worldwide: Update from the 13th International Conference on AIDS.

Martin, V.,Cayla, J. A., Moris, M. L., Alonso, L. E., Perez R. 1998. Predictive Factors of HIV infection in Injection Drug Users Upon Incarceration. *Journal of Epidemiology.* June 998. Vol. 14. No. 4. Pages 327-33.

Maruschak, L. M. "HIV in Prisons, 2007-08". Bureau of Justice Statistic. U.S. Department of Justice. Office of Justice Program. Bureau of Justice Statistics. December 2009, NCJ. 228307

Maruschak, Laura M. 2004. "HIV in Prisons 2001."Bureau of Justice Statistics Bulitin.
U.S. Department of Justice. Office of Justice Program. Bureau of Justice Statistics. January 2001.

MacMillian et al, (1997); In Understanding the Complexity of Childhood Sexual Abuse: A Review of the Literature With Implications for Family Counseling. Hunter, S. V. The Family Journal. October 2006. Vol. 14. No. 4. Pages 349-358.

McMullen, Richie J. 1990. *Male Rape: Breaking the Silence on the Last Taboo.* London: GMP Publishers Ltd.

Mezey, G. C. and King, M. 1989. "Effects of sexual assault on men: A survey of 22 victims." *Psychological Medicine* 19: 2005-2009.

Mezey and King, (1989) in Perception of male victims in depicted sexual assaults: A review of the literature. *Aggression and Violent Behavior.* Volume 11, Issue 4, July-August 2006. Pages 367-377.

Minton, T.D. AND Sabol, W. J. "Jail Inmates at Midyear 2008". Bureau of Justice Statistics. U.S. Department of Justice. Office of Justice Program. Statistical Table. March 2009, NCJ 225709

Mitchell, D., Richard, H. and Gordon, N. 1999. "Attributes of victims responsibility, pleasure, and trauma in male rape." *The Journal of Sex Research* 36: 369-73.

Moore, Q. 2007. "Blacks need to pay more attention to sexual assaults." *The Washington Informer* 43 (24): 38.

Nalavany, B. and Abell, N. 2004. "An initial validation of measure of personal and social perception of the sexual abuse of males." *Research on Social Work Practice* 14 (5): 368-78.

O'Brien, D. 2005. *The cries of men: voices of Jamaican men who have been rape and sexually abused.* Bloomington, IN: iUniverse.

Okie, S. "The Problem of Prison Rape" study conducted in 2004. *Stop Prison Rape Fact Sheet.* October 2007.

Struckman, C, and Struckman, D. In Men's Reaction to Female Coercion. *Psychiatric Times.* Vol. 17. No. 3. March 1, 2001.

Herek, G. M. 2004. "Beyond "Homophobia": Thinking About Sexual Prejudice and Stigma in the Twentt-First Century. *Sexuality Research and Social Policy. Journal of NSRC.* April. 2004. Vol. 1. No. 2.

Powell, C. 1990. "Male rape victims; Help for an underreported abuse. *The Washington Post.*

Prison Rape Elimination Act, 2003 (42 U.S.C. 15601 (13), 15602(1).

Rebic, G. 1996, 7 March. "Silent Victims of a Pathological Aggressor." *Vecernji List.* http://www.cdsp.neu.edu/info/students/marko/vecernji/vecernji1.html.

Redman, P. 2000. "In Tarred with the Same Brush: 'Homophobia' and the Role of the Unconscious in School-based Cultures of Masculinity". *Sexualities* 2000. Volume 3. Number 4. Pages. 83-99 The online version of this article can be found at: http://sex.sagepub.com/content/3/4/483

Renold (2007). In Hartil, M. The Sexual Abuse of Boys in Organized Male Sports. *Men and Masculinity.* October 2009. Vol. 12. No. 2. Pages 225-249

Rogers, P. 1998. In "Male Sexual assault victims: A selective review of the literature and implications of support services."Davies, Michelle. 2002. *Aggression and Violent Behavior* 7(3), May-June 2002: 2003-2214.

Shechory, M. and Idisis, Yael. Rape Myths and Social distance toward sex offenders and victims among therapist and students. *Sex Roles: A Journal of Research.* Vol. 54: 9-10, 651-658. May 1, (2006).

Scott A. Allen, *et al.* 2003. "Hepatitis C Among Offenders—Correctional Challenge and Public Health Opportunity," Federal Probation. Vol. 67. No. 2. September 2003

Seabrook, J. 1990. "Power lust." *New Statesman and Society* 98 : 20.

Sharpe, J., Selley, C., Low, L, and Hall, Z. 2001. "Group analytic therapy for male survivors of childhood sexual abuse." *The Group-Analytic Society. June 2001. Vol. 34. No. 2. Pages* 195-209

Siegal, J. The Relationship between Child Sexual Abuse and Female Delinquency and Crime: A Prospective Study. Journal of Research in Crime and Delinquency. February 2003. Vol. 40. No. 1 Pages 71-94.

Simons, L, Callie, B and Ronald, S (2008). *A Test of Explanations for the Effects of Harsh Parenting on the Perpetration of Dating Violence and Sexual Coercion Among College Males. Violence and Victims. Vol. 23.* Issue. 1. Pages 66-82.

Sivakumaran, Sandesh. 2005. "Male/male rape and the taint of homosexuality." *Human Rights Quarterly* 27: 1274-1306.

———. 2007. "Sexual Violence Against Men in Armed Conflict." *European Journal of International Law* 18 (2):253-76

Skjelsbæk, I. 2001. "Sexual Violence in Times of War: A New Challenge for Peace Operations?" *International Peacekeeping*, 8: 2.

Stone, R. 2004. *No Secrets No Lies*. New York: Broadway Books.

Stop Prison Rape. http://spr.igc.org/en/survivorstories/main.html

Struckman-Johnson, Cindy, and Struckman-Johnson, David. 2000. "No Escape: Male Rape in U.S. Prisons." *The Prison Journal* 80(4, December 2000):379-90.

———. 2000, "Sexual Coercion Rates in Seven Midwestern Prison Facilities for Men." *The Prison Journal* 80(4, December 2000): 379-90. Available at http://www.spr.org/pdf/struckman.pdf.

———. 2002. "Sexual Coercion Reported by Women in Three Midwestern Prison" *J. Sex Res* 39: 217, 220.

Struckman-Johnson, Cindy and Struckman-Johnson, David, "A comparison of Sexual Coercion Experiences Reported by Men and Women in Prison," 21, Journal of Interpersonal Violence 1531, 1599 (2006)

Struckman-Johnson, Cindy, *et al.* 1996."Sexual Coercion Reported by Men and Women in Prison." *J. Sex Res.* 33:67.

Susan Okie (2007). Sex, Drugs, Prisons and HIV, 356 *New England Journal of Medicine* 105 (2007).

Tewksbury, R. 2007. "Effects of sexual assaults on men: physical, mental and sexual consequences". *International Journal of Men's Health*. Vol. 6. No. 1. Pages 22-35. Spring. May 15, 2007.

Thornhil, R. and Palmer, C. 2000. "Why men rape." *The Sciences* 40 (1): 30.

Tickner, J. A. 1992. *Gender in International Relations.* New York: Columbia University Press.

Trent, M., Clum, G., and, Roche, K. 2007. "Sexual victimization and reproductive health outcomes in urban youths." *Ambulatory Pediatrics* 7 (4):313-16.

Walker, J., Archer, J., and Davies, M. 2005. "Effects of rape on men: A descriptive analysis." *Archives of Sexual Behaviors* 34 (1): 69-80.

Walmsley, R. 2003. *Global Incarceration and Prison Trends.* Forum on Crime and Society.

Watney, (1987) p. 47. In Tarred with the Same Brush: 'Homophobia' and the Role of the Unconscious in School-based Cultures of Masculinity by Peter Redman. Sexualities 2000. Volume 3. Number 4. 483 The online version of this article can be found at: http://sex.sagepub.com/content/3/4/483

Webb, W. J. 2001. *Slaves, Women and Homosexuals.* Leicester: Intervarsity Press.

Welch, Michael. (1997). Violence Against Women by Professional Football Players: A Gender Analysis of Hypermasculinity, Positional Status, Narcissism, and Entitlement. Journal of Sports and Social Issues. November 1997. Vol. 21. No. 4 Pages 392-411

Whitebeck and Hoyt, (1999). Event History Analysis of Antecedents to Running Away from Home and Being on the Street. American Behavioral Scientist. September 2001 Vol. 45. Pages 51-65.

Sivakumaran, S. 2007. "Sexual Violence Against Men in Armed Conflicts." *The European Journal of International Law. Volume* 18. Number 2. Pages 255-276

Willis, D.G. "Male-on-Male Rape of an Adult Man: A Case Review and Implications for Interventions" by Danny G. Willis. *Journal of the American Psychiatric Nurses Association* 14 (6, December/January 2009): 454-61

Whitebeck, L., Hoyt, D., Johnson, K., and Chen, X. 2007. "Victimization and posttraumatic stress disorder among runaway and homeless adolescents." *Violence and Victims* 22 (6): 721-34.
New York City Alliance Against Sexual Assault. 2008. Fact sheets: Male rape.

UN Office on Drugs and Crime, 2006. "HIV Prevention, Care, Treatment and Support in Prison Settings A Framework for an Effective National Response."

UNAIDS. 2006. *AIDS Epidemic Update.* Geneva, UNAIDS.

UNODC-UNAIDS-WHO. 2006. *Framework for HIV AIDS Prevention, Treatment and Care in Prison*

US Centers for Disease Control and Prevention. 2002. Prison Rape Spreading Deadly Diseases.

United Nations Website

http://search.un.org/search?ie=utf8&andsite=un_org&andoutput=xml_no_dtd&andclient=UN_Website_English&andnum=10&andlr=lang_en&andproxystylesheet=UN_Website_en&andoe=utf8&andq=definition+of+sexual+abuse

http://www.ncvc.org/ncvc/main.aspx?dbName=DocumentViewer&andDocumentID=32369

Medical and social aspects of sexual assault of males: a survey of 100 victims—*The Houston Chronicle* 16 October 2005.

Myths about sexual assault: http://www.menweb.org/sexamyth.htm

The Health Status of Soon-to-be-Released Inmates: A Report to Congress. National Commission on Correctional Health Care, March 2002. http://www.ncchc.org/pubs/pubs_stbr.html

American Psychiatric Association's *Diagnostic and Statistical Manual of Mental Disorders* (Fourth Edition) for her article,

New York City Alliance Against Rape and Sexual Assault http://www. svfreenyc.org/